JUNIOR LEVEL

Name: Abu Bakr.

Age:

Class:

Markaz Mu'aadh Bin Jabal

Islamic Studies Syllabus

Markaz Mu'aadh bin Jabal,
19 Spackmans Way, Slough, SL1 2SA, UK

+44 (0)1753 533 376

info@markazmuaadh.com

www.markazmuaadh.com

Ordering Information:
Wholesale discounts are available for schools, Masaajid and bookshops. For details, please contact us at the above address.

Second edition: 1445AH/October 2023

Markaz Mu'aadh Bin Jabal

TABLE OF CONTENTS

‘AQEEDAH

Islām
&
Eemān

بسم الله الرحمن الرحيم

Knowledge of Allāh, His Messenger and Islām

We obtain knowledge of Allāh, His Messenger ﷺ and Islām from **revelation** that came from Allāh, which are two sources.

The Qur'ān	The Speech of Allāh, **<u>NOT</u>** created.
The Hadeeth	The sayings, actions and silent approvals of the Prophet Muhammad ﷺ – which are collectively known as the Sunnah.

Both the Qur'ān and Sunnah are revelation. They MUST be understood with the understanding of the Sahaabah (Companions) of Allāh's Messenger ﷺ. This is because Allāh commanded us in the Qur'ān to follow the way and understanding of the Sahaabah and the Prophet Muhammad ﷺ told us to follow their way. In addition, when the Qur'ān was being revealed to the Prophet Muhammad ﷺ, **who was present and witnessing how the Prophet Muhammad ﷺ was acting upon the verses of Allāh?**

It was the Sahaabah of the Prophet Muhammad ﷺ.

That is why we follow Islām as they understood it.

Tawheed

Tawheed is the most important aspect of our life and the foundation of our religion. Tawheed means to believe in the Oneness of Allāh in His Lordship, Worship and Names and Attributes. Whoever learns and acts upon Tawheed without committing Shirk (making partners with Allāh) and major sins, then he will be from the successful ones and is promised Jannah (Paradise) in the Ākhirah (Hereafter).

A person who acts upon Tawheed but falls short in doing many good deeds is better than those who do not act upon Tawheed but do many good deeds, because Tawheed is the foundation of our religion and the reason for our creation.

To achieve this great reward we will learn what Tawheed is and its three categories inshaa'Allāh.

1. Tawheed ar-Rubboobiyyah

It is to know with certainty that the only Lord is **Allāh** Who creates from nothing. He gives His creation food, drink and many other things for them to survive. Allāh controls everything from the rain, day, night, life, death and many other things.

Who is your Lord (Rabb)?

Who created you?

Who is the One who gives you food and drink?

Who is the One who gave you everything to help you to stay alive?

Allāh created us, He created our parents and our friends. He created everything that we see and that which we do not see. Allāh gave us so many blessings that we cannot count them. It is Allāh Who provided for us food and air whilst we were in the bellies of our mothers. He took care of our needs when we could not even speak and even if we were able to, no one would hear us. He gave us these things so that we can use them to worship Him alone and to know Him, so that we may become good Muslims!

Allāh created everything, He created the sky above us, the sun, which gives us light, heat and many other benefits, Allāh created the moon, the millions of stars. He created the night that we may sleep and rest after our activities during the day.

He created all the oceans, seas, rivers and all the different creatures that live therein, that have different colours and sizes.

Think about all the different types of animals, different sizes, shapes and different colours. Some having more than one colour, some walk on their bellies, some walk on two legs while some on four.

Name four Sūrahs in the Qur'ān named after an animal.

Name four animals that walk on two legs

Name four animals that walk on four legs

Allāh created the mountains, the many different types of birds that fly and their different colours. Who holds them up? Allāh!

When you see these beautiful creations, think, reflect and remember who created them? Allāh!

Allāh gave us rain which comes from above. With this rain, fields get watered, the fruits and vegetables grow, the flowers grow and become beautiful and animals drink from this rain.

Allāh gave us our eyes so that we can see His beautiful creation, ears so we can hear different sounds and a tongue to talk to each other, hands so that we may pick up things, eat and drink with them, legs so that we may walk and play. He gave us the air so that we can breathe. He is so kind to us.

We love Allāh and thank Him by doing what He tells us to do and stay away from that which He tells us to stay away from. Allāh only tells us to stay away from things because they are not good for us and when He tells us to do something, He only tells us because it is good for us.

Tawheed ar-Rubbobiyyah is to single out Allāh in His actions.

أَمْ خُلِقُوا۟ مِنْ غَيْرِ شَىْءٍ أَمْ هُمُ ٱلْخَٰلِقُونَ

Were they created by nothing? Or did they create themselves?

(at-Toor:35)

ٱللَّهُ خَٰلِقُ كُلِّ شَىْءٍ

Allāh is the Creator of all things.

(az-Zumar:62)

ٱلَّذِىٓ أَحْسَنَ كُلَّ شَىْءٍ خَلَقَهُۥ

(Allāh) Who perfected everything, which He created.

(as-Sajdah:7)

ٱقْرَأْ بِٱسْمِ رَبِّكَ ٱلَّذِى خَلَقَ ﴿١﴾ خَلَقَ ٱلْإِنسَٰنَ مِنْ عَلَقٍ ﴿٢﴾ ٱقْرَأْ وَرَبُّكَ ٱلْأَكْرَمُ ﴿٣﴾

ٱلَّذِى عَلَّمَ بِٱلْقَلَمِ ﴿٤﴾ عَلَّمَ ٱلْإِنسَٰنَ مَا لَمْ يَعْلَمْ ﴿٥﴾

Read! In the Name of your Lord, Who has created (all that exists) (1) He has created man from a clot (blood) (2) Read! And your Lord is the Most Generous (3) Who has taught (the writing) by the pen (4) He has taught man that which he knew not (5)

(al-'Alaq:1-5)

لَقَدْ خَلَقْنَا ٱلْإِنسَٰنَ فِىٓ أَحْسَنِ تَقْوِيمٍ

Indeed, We created man in the best of forms.

(at-Teen:4)

2. Tawheed al-Asmaa' wa-Sifaat

It is the belief that Allāh alone is the sole possessor of perfection in every sense, nothing from His creation has any share whatsoever in this.

We love Him because He made us Muslims and we only worship Him, the Creator. We do not worship that which is created, be it humans, stones, trees, the sun, the moon and the other created things. We worship Allāh alone, the Creator of everything.

- Who should we worship?
- Are we allowed to worship the creation?
- Write down the things which you see with your eyes that Allāh created.

We love Allāh because He has the most beautiful Names. He is al-Baseer (The One who sees everything) and nothing is hidden from Him. Even if there was a very small stone in the mountains, Allāh sees it. The black ant, which is upon a black stone in the dark night, Allāh sees it. Allāh knows what is in our hearts and what we think.

He is as-Samee' (the All-Hearer), even if you whispered in the corner of a room to your friend, Allāh hears it. Even if all the people in the world were to speak at the same time in different languages, Allāh will hear everything and He will be able to give them whatever they asked for.

He is al-'Aleem (the All-Knowing), His knowledge encompasses everything, He is the only One who knows what will happen in the future. He knows what has happened in the past; there is not a leaf anywhere in the world except that He knows when and where it falls.

He is ar-Razzaaq (the Great Provider). He gave us our food, drink, clothes, our parents, our houses and everything. When someone has done good to you, how happy do you become with that person? And how much do you thank them? What about Allāh? He has given us everything so that we can live, be healthy and be happy. Shouldn't we give Him the most thanks by worshipping Him alone and doing everything that He tells us to do because He knows what is good for us? And to stay away from the bad things because Allāh knows what is bad for us.

When we know that Allāh can hear everything and see everything, when we know that He is so kind and He gives us so many things then we in turn should only ask Allāh alone for our needs. We do not ask a dead person, an angel, an idol, or a tree because they are created and cannot benefit us nor answer our needs.

Tawheed al-Asmaa' wa-Sifaat is to single out Allāh with His most beautiful Names & lofty Attributes. The following are some of our Lord's most beautiful and perfect Names and Attributes.

الْعَزِيـزُ The Almighty	اَلْعَلِـيْمُ The All-Knowing	الْحَيُّ The Perfect Living
الرَّزَّاقُ The Great Provider	الْخَالِـقُ The Creator and Maker of Everything	السَّلَامُ The Flawless One
الأَوَّلُ The First	الآخِرُ The Last	الْجَبَّـارُ The Exalted and Almighty Compeller
الإِلَهُ The One Who Alone Deserves to be Worshipped	الأَعْلَى The Most High	الشَّـاكِرُ The Appreciative

ٱلْحَقُّ
The True One

الرَّؤُوفُ
The Compassionate and Kind

الأَكْرَمُ
The Most Generous

الصَّمَدُ
The Perfect Lord and Master Upon Whom All of the Creation Depends

العَظِيمُ
The Magnificient

ٱلْحَفِيظُ
The Guardian and Preserver

التَّوَّابُ
The One Who Guides His Servants to Repent and Accepts Their Repentance Again and Again

العَفُوُّ
The One Who Pardons Again and Again

الحَمِيدُ
The One Who is Deservedly Praised

الحَافِظُ
The Protector

الخَبِيرُ
The Fully Aware

الشَّهِيدُ
The Witness

Allāh has more than 99 Names & Attributes as mentioned in the Qur'ān and Sunnah. Whoever memorises these and practices what they entail and calls upon Allāh with them will enter Jannah.

Memorise 30 Names of Allāh with their meanings.

قُلْ هُوَ ٱللَّهُ أَحَدٌ ﴿١﴾ ٱللَّهُ ٱلصَّمَدُ ﴿٢﴾ لَمْ يَلِدْ وَلَمْ يُولَدْ ﴿٣﴾ وَلَمْ يَكُن لَّهُۥ كُفُوًا أَحَدٌۢ ﴿٤﴾

Say (O Muhammad ﷺ): He is Allāh, (The) One and Unique. (1) Allāh the Self-Sufficient Master, Whom all creatures need, (He neither eats nor drinks). (2) He did not have a child, nor was He born to someone else. (3) And there is none that can be equal to Him or comparable to Him. (4) (al-Ikhlās:1-4)

3. Tawheed al-Uloohiyyah

The reason behind the creation of the humans and the jinn is for them to worship Allāh alone without associating any partners. When we make Du'ā we only make it to Allāh directly, because He is the only One Who knows and can respond to all our needs. When we pray, our prayers are only for Allāh alone. When we seek protection from any harm, we seek it from Allāh alone because He has power over all things.

We do not wear any type of string, ring, bracelet or talisman to protect us. To wear these things for protection and good luck is not allowed in Islām and is Shirk. The people who worship idols or other than Allāh do not believe that these things created them or created the universe, but rather they believed that the idols which they worshipped would bring them closer to Allāh. However, this is wrong and it is **Shirk**.

When we are on a journey, be it on a plane or a ship and it starts to shake and swing about in the air due to the wind or waves, we should call upon Allāh directly to rescue us, **no-one** else, not even a Prophet, angel or anyone from the creation. If we did call upon other than Allāh, this will be Shirk which is the greatest sin one can do.

Allāh sent Prophets to call the people to His worship alone and to stay away from worshipping everything else. Allāh wants the people to be upon the right way and not to do evil things. And Allāh does not like that you worship others besides Him.

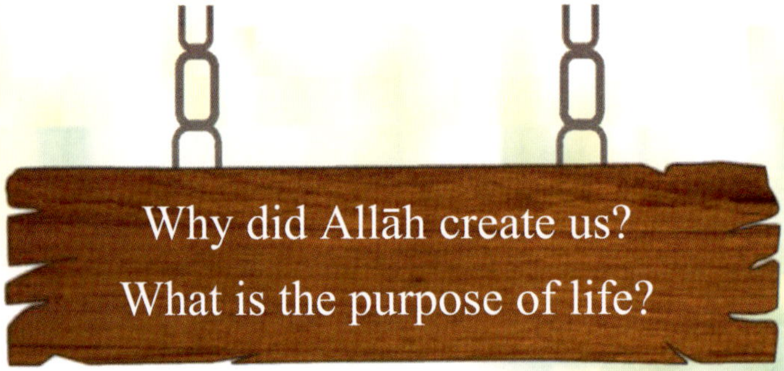

The purpose of our life is to worship Allāh alone and to know Him.

The proof is the Saying of Allāh:

وَمَا خَلَقْتُ الْجِنَّ وَالْإِنسَ إِلَّا لِيَعْبُدُونِ

And I did not create jinn and mankind, except that they should worship Me (alone). (adh-Dhāriyāt:56)

فَاعْلَمْ أَنَّهُ لَآ إِلَٰهَ إِلَّا اللَّهُ

Know that none has the right to be worshipped except Allāh. (Muhammad:19)

This is known as Tawheed al-Uloohiyyah (to single out Allāh in worship). This is to single out Allāh with our actions (like Praying, Fasting, Hajj, making Du'ā, reading the Qur'ān etc). This is the right of Allāh, which only belongs to Him, no-one else.

يَٰٓأَيُّهَا النَّاسُ اعْبُدُوا رَبَّكُمُ الَّذِى خَلَقَكُمْ وَالَّذِينَ مِن قَبْلِكُمْ لَعَلَّكُمْ تَتَّقُونَ

O mankind! Single out your Lord with all worship, He Who created you and all those came before you, so that you may be of those who are pious. (al-Baqarah:21)

وَإِلَٰهُكُمْ إِلَٰهٌ وَاحِدٌ

And the God alone who has the right to be worshipped is a single God (Allāh) (al-Baqarah:163)

وَقَالَ الْمَسِيحُ يَٰبَنِىٓ إِسْرَٰٓءِيلَ اعْبُدُوا اللَّهَ رَبِّى وَرَبَّكُمْ

But the Messiah 'Isa (Jesus) said: "O Children of Israel! Worship Allāh, my Lord and your Lord." (al-Māidah:72)

Summary

To believe with certainty that Allāh is the only Lord of creation, He alone is their provider and sustainer. Allāh has Names and Attributes that none of the creation share and Allāh is to be singled out for worship alone. Tawheed is maintaining the Oneness of Allāh in all the above-mentioned categories. Islām makes a clear distinction between the Creator and the created.

The only way to true happiness in this life and in the Hereafter is by worshipping Allāh alone as He prescribed by following His Messenger ﷺ.

Where is Allāh?

- Allāh is the Creator of everything.
- There is nothing like Him.
- He is greater than all of creation.

He is not inside His creation, so **where is Allāh?** We can only answer this with what Allāh and His Prophet Muhammad ﷺ have informed us. Allāh is where He, the Most High, has told us in His Noble Book:

الرَّحْمَٰنُ عَلَى الْعَرْشِ اسْتَوَىٰ

"The Most Merciful is above His Throne (in a manner that befits His Majesty)".
(Ta-Ha:5)

سَبِّحِ اسْمَ رَبِّكَ الْأَعْلَى

Glorify the Name of your Lord, the Most High.
(al-A'lā:1)

Allāh is above His Throne in a way that befits His Greatness and Majesty. Allāh is higher than all of the creation. There is nothing above Him, He is above the mountains, stars, sky, the heavens and the Throne. Even though Allāh is above all of His creation, He still Hears, Knows and Sees everything in the creation, nothing is hidden from Him.

What is Islām?

Islām is the religion of every Prophet and it is to worship Allāh alone. Those who follow Islām are called Muslims.

Islām is:

- Submission and surrender to the will of Allāh
- Acting upon Allāh's obedience
- Staying away from Shirk

What are the 5 pillars of Islām?

Islām is built upon 5 pillars.

1. Shahadah	It is the statement, "There is none worthy of worship in truth except Allāh alone and to testify that Muhammad ﷺ is the Messenger of Allāh", which, when said with certainty, truthfulness and sincerity enters you into Islām.
2. Salāh	To pray 5 times a day.
3. Zakaah	To give 1/40 (2.5%) of your yearly savings to the poor.
4. Sawm	To fast the month of Ramadān.

5. Hajj	To perform the pilgrimage to Makkah once in your lifetime if you have the financial means and health to do so.

What is Eemān (Faith)?

Eemān is:

- Belief in the heart
- Speech upon the tongue
- Action of the limbs

It increases with obedience to Allāh and it decreases with disobedience (sinning).

Belief in the heart

Includes the six pillars of Eemān and everything that Allāh and His Messenger ﷺ have informed us of.

Speech upon the tongue

To pronounce the Shahadah, saying good words and remembering Allāh with statements like saying Subhan Allāh, Alhumdulillaah, Allāhu Akbar etc, saying the Adhān (call to prayer), reciting Qur'ān and speaking the truth.

Actions of the limbs

The prayer, walking to the mosque, Hajj, helping your parents, helping those in need, removing harmful things, making Wudhu and keeping yourself clean.

What are the 6 pillars of Eemān?

1. Eemān in Allāh
2. Eemān in the Angels
3. Eemān in His Books
4. Eemān in His Prophets and Messengers
5. Eemān in the Last Day
6. Eemān in Pre-Decree (the good and the bad)

1. Eemān in Allāh

The first pillar of Eemān is to believe with certainty that Allāh is our Lord, the One who controls everything that exists and that He provides for all of His creation.

He is the One who gives life and death. It is to believe with certainty that Allāh has beautiful Names and lofty Attributes and there is nothing like Him.

He is al-Ahad - The Unique. The One Who is Alone and Unique in every sense. He has no child nor was He born. He is al-Qayyoom - The One Who sustains everything that exists. The One who has no need of anything whatsoever, but rather everything is in need of Him to exist.

Allāh, the One who possesses the Most perfect and complete Attributes is the One deserving of **all** worship.

He is al-Awwal - The First, Who was before everything without any beginning, and He is al-Aakhir - The Last, the One Who remains after everything else, without any end.

He is al-Hayy - The Ever-Living Who always remains without a beginning or an end, with perfect and Everlasting Life, Who never dies.

2. Eemān in the Angels

The second pillar of Eemān is to believe with certainty in the existence of angels. They are a creation which are created from light, they were created before the humans. There are some whose names we know, for example Jibrā'īl, Mikā'īl and Isrāfīl and many whose names we do not know.

The angels have wings but we do not know what they look like. They have certain duties that Allāh has given them, for example the duty of Jibrā'īl is to bring down the revelation from Allāh to the Prophets, the duty of Mikā'īl is to move the clouds and the duty of Isrāfīl is to blow the Horn which will take place at the end of time. The angels never disobey Allāh.

3. Eemān in the Books

The third pillar of Eemān is to believe with certainty that Allāh sent Books to the Prophets, these Books contained guidance for the people. The Books that we know of by name are; Suhuf (Scripture) of Ibrāhīm عليه السلام, Zabūr (Psalms) which was revealed to Prophet Dāwūd عليه السلام, Taurah (Torah) to Prophet Mūsa عليه السلام, Injeel (Gospel) to Prophet 'Isa عليه السلام and The Qur'ān which is the final Book which was revealed to Prophet Muhammad ﷺ. The previous nations changed and corrupted the Books that Allāh had revealed to them except The Qur'ān, which Allāh has promised to protect from any corruption, distortion or change. The Books of Allāh are the Speech of Allāh.

4. Eemān in the Prophets of Allāh

The fourth pillar of Eemān is to believe with certainty that Allāh sent Prophets to the people as a guide, to show the people:

1. How to worship Allāh
2. What Allāh hates so that they can stay away from it
3. What He is pleased with so that they can carry it out

There are some Prophets whose names we know and some that we do not know. The following are the Prophets that are mentioned in the Qur'ān:

Prophets of Allāh

Ādam عليه السلام	Idrees عليه السلام	Nūh عليه السلام
Hūd عليه السلام	Sālih عليه السلام	Ibrāhīm عليه السلام
Lūt عليه السلام	Shu'ayb عليه السلام	Ismā'īl عليه السلام
Ishāq عليه السلام	Ya'qūb عليه السلام	Yūsuf عليه السلام
Ayyūb عليه السلام	Dhul Kifl عليه السلام	Yūnus عليه السلام
Mūsa عليه السلام	Harūn عليه السلام	'Isa عليه السلام
Dāwūd عليه السلام	Sulaymān عليه السلام	'Uzayr عليه السلام
Zakariyya عليه السلام	Yahyā عليه السلام	Ilyās عليه السلام
	Muhammad ﷺ	

All the Prophets were human beings, they drank, they ate, they fell ill, most of them married and had children. The Prophets do not share any of the Attributes of Allāh. The first Prophet was Ādam عليه السلام who was created without a mother and a father. The Prophet 'Isa عليه السلام was created without a father but with a mother and **he is a servant of Allāh** NOT the son of Allāh. The last Prophet is the Prophet Muhammad ﷺ, there is no Prophet after him.

5. Eemān in the Last Day

The fifth pillar of Eemān is to believe with certainty that Allāh will bring everyone back to life and will hold them to account. Part of this pillar is to believe with certainty about certain events that will occur, from them is the questioning of the grave in which every person will be asked three questions.

1. Who is your Lord?
2. What is your religion?
3. Who was your Prophet?

Those who answer correctly will be rewarded in their graves and those who do not answer correctly will be punished.

We must also believe other events leading up to the Day of Judgement.

I. Angel Isrāfīl will blow the Horn and this will cause everyone who is living at that time to die.
II. The second blowing will bring everyone back to life.
III. Then the people will be judged for what they used to do in this life.
IV. The smallest of good deeds and bad deeds will be judged and be placed on the Scales.
V. The Scales will weigh our deeds, our book of records and us.

VI. After this weighing will be the crossing over the Bridge which is over the Hell-Fire. This Bridge is finer than a strand of hair and sharper than a sword.

VII. People will cross it at different speeds, some will fall off and into the Hell-Fire. The speed at which you cross will depend on your Eemān and your deeds in this life.

Finally, those who enter Paradise will live there forever in happiness, they will never die, nor get sick or bored and they will have whatever they wish.

As for the people of the Hell-Fire, they will enter it due to what they did in this life from disbelief and sins and they will be punished.

May Allāh protect us and our families from the punishment of the Hell-Fire. (Āmeen)

6. Eemān in Pre-Decree

It is to believe in the Qadar (Pre-Decree of Allāh).

I. We believe as Muslims that Allāh has always known everything and nothing is hidden from Him.

II. He knows everything from the beginning to the end.

III. Whether good happens or bad, Allāh always knows before it occurs.

Allāh has given us the ability, intellect and likewise sent Books and Messengers to show us what is right and what is wrong. If we do bad, it is because we chose to. However, when we do bad we should regret it and ask Allāh to forgive us and try our best not to repeat that bad deed. And if we do good it is because Allāh blessed us and gave us the ability to do so, this is why we should thank Him when we carry out good deeds and when Allāh protects us from doing bad things.

The worst sin (Shirk)

إِنَّ الشِّرْكَ لَظُلْمٌ عَظِيمٌ

Indeed, associating others in worship alongside Allāh is great injustice. (Sūrah Luqmān:13)

Allāh is the One Who created us, brought us into existence when we were nothing, took care of us when we were in the belly of our mother, gave us hearing, sight, limbs, and many other blessings. He gave us these so that we may worship Him alone and to see who does the best actions.

Worship of Allāh alone is the purpose of life, worshipping Him alone is a sign of being grateful to Him, so the worst belief or action one can do is that which contains Shirk.

Shirk is to make a partner with Allāh in His Ruboobiyyah (Lordship) or His Uloohiyyah (Worship) or His Asmaa Wa Sifaat (Names and Attributes).

We will give an example, Allāh has given you clothing, your house, your food, your good health, clean water to drink and to bathe and many other things. However you offer an act of worship to one who themselves are in need of Allāh for the same blessings as you.

This is no doubt the greatest of all sins. We should make all of our worship purely and sincerely for our Creator, the One Who provides for us and all of His creation. He is the One Who hears and responds to the needs of His creation. We should make Du'ā to the One Who heard the Du'ā of Prophet Yunus (May Allāh honour and protect him), who was in the belly of a whale, in the lowest depths of the sea and in darkness and Allāh heard and responded to his Du'ā. All the Prophets made Du'a directly to Allāh alone and they told their people to do the same.

Shirk ar-Ruboobiyyah: To believe that there is someone besides Allāh who creates from nothing, or has control over the creation.

Shirk Uloohiyyah: To offer any act of worship to other than Allāh, for example making du'ā to other than Allāh, to seek help with others besides Allāh, in that which only Allāh can help with.

Shirk in Asmaa wa-Sifaat: To make Allāh similar to creation or the creation similar to Allāh.

The conditions for an act of worship to be accepted

1. **Ikhlās** (Sincerity)

That you do the action only for the sake of Allāh alone, seeking His reward, without having Shirk in it. You do not do any act of worship to show off, nor to seek the praise of the people nor to seek any worldly benefit. Allāh will not accept any action which is not done with sincerity.

2. **Mutaaba'a** (Following the Sunnah of the Final Prophet Muhammad ﷺ).

We only know what Allāh loves and is pleased with by way of the Qur'ān and the Sunnah of the Prophet Muhammad ﷺ. Allāh, from His kindness and mercy did not leave it to any of us to choose how we worship Him, rather He sent the best of His creation - Prophet Muhammad ﷺ to show us how to worship Him. A sign that you love Allāh is that you worship Him as the Prophet Muhammad ﷺ worshipped Him.

If this condition is missing then the action becomes an innovation (Bid'ah).

What is the Sunnah?

The Sunnah is the way or methodology of Prophet Muhammad ﷺ in belief, worship and manners.

There are four types of Sunnah

1. Qawliyyah	What Prophet Muhammad ﷺ said.
2. Fi'leeyah	What Prophet Muhammad ﷺ did.
3. Taqreeriyyah	What Prophet Muhammad ﷺ approved of.
4. Wasfiyyah	His attributes and noble manners.

Following the Sunnah is the only way to truly worship Allāh as He wants us to.

Āyāt to Memorise

1. What is the purpose of life?

And I did not create jinn and mankind, except that they should worship Me (alone). (adh-Dhariyāt:56)

وَمَا خَلَقْتُ الْجِنَّ وَالْإِنسَ إِلَّا لِيَعْبُدُونِ

2. What was the call of the Prophets and Messengers?

We sent a Messenger to every nation, ordering them that they should worship Allāh alone, obey Him and make their worship purely for Him, and that they should stay away from everything which is worshipped besides Allāh. (an-Nahl:36)

وَلَقَدْ بَعَثْنَا فِي كُلِّ أُمَّةٍ رَّسُولًا أَنِ اعْبُدُوا اللَّهَ وَاجْتَنِبُوا الطَّاغُوتَ

3. Proof for the 5 pillars of Islām:

a) Shahadah

I. (1st part of Shahadah – La ilaaha illa-Allāh)

Allāh bears witness that none has the right to be worshipped but He, and the angels, and those having knowledge (also give this witness), (He always) maintains His creation in Justice. None has the right to be worshipped but He), the Almighty, the All-Wise. (Āali-Imrān:18)

شَهِدَ اللَّهُ أَنَّهُ لَا إِلَٰهَ إِلَّا هُوَ وَالْمَلَائِكَةُ وَأُولُو الْعِلْمِ قَائِمًا بِالْقِسْطِ ۚ لَا إِلَٰهَ إِلَّا هُوَ الْعَزِيزُ الْحَكِيمُ

II. (2nd part of Shahadah – Muhammad-ur-Rasoolullah)

"Muhammad ﷺ is not the father of any of your men, but he is the Messenger of Allāh and the last of the Prophets." (al-Ahzāb:40)

مَّا كَانَ مُحَمَّدٌ أَبَا أَحَدٍ مِّن رِّجَالِكُمْ وَلَٰكِن رَّسُولَ اللَّهِ

وَخَاتَمَ النَّبِيِّينَ

b) Salāh & Zakah

And they were not commanded except that they should worship Allāh alone, making their worship and obedience purely for Him, upon the true religion and free from Shirk; and that they should establish the prayer, pay the Zakaat (obligatory charity) and that is the upright and true religion. (al-Bayyinah:5)

وَمَآ أُمِرُوٓا إِلَّا لِيَعْبُدُوا اللَّهَ مُخْلِصِينَ لَهُ الدِّينَ حُنَفَآءَ وَيُقِيمُوا الصَّلَاةَ وَيُؤْتُوا الزَّكَاةَ وَذَٰلِكَ دِينُ الْقَيِّمَةِ

c) Fasting (Sawm)

O you who believe! Fasting is prescribed as an obligation for you as it was prescribed as an obligation for those who came before you, so that you may attain Taqwa (obedience to Allāh and avoidance of whatever He has forbidden). (al-Baqarah:183)

يَآ أَيُّهَا الَّذِينَ آمَنُوا كُتِبَ عَلَيْكُمُ الصِّيَامُ كَمَا كُتِبَ عَلَى الَّذِينَ مِنْ قَبْلِكُمْ لَعَلَّكُمْ تَتَّقُونَ

d) Hajj

And Hajj to Allāh's sacred House (K'abah) is an obligation upon those able to perform it, and whoever refuses and rejects the obligation of Hajj to Allāh's house, then Allāh has no need of him or of any of the creation. (Āali-Imrān:97)

وَلِلَّهِ عَلَى النَّاسِ حِجُّ الْبَيْتِ مَنِ اسْتَطَاعَ إِلَيْهِ سَبِيلًا وَمَنْ كَفَرَ فَإِنَّ اللَّهَ غَنِيٌّ عَنِ الْعَالَمِينَ

4. Proof of 3 categories of Tawheed

I. Tawheed ar-Rubboobiyyah

All the praise is for Allāh, the Lord of all creation (al-Fātihah:2)

الْحَمْدُ لِلَّهِ رَبِّ الْعَالَمِينَ

II. Tawheed al-Uloohiyyah

And your ilaah (God) is One ilaah (God - Allāh), there is none who has the right to be worshipped but He, the Most Merciful, the Bestower of Mercy. (al-Baqarah:163)

وَإِلَـٰهُكُمْ إِلَـٰهٌ وَاحِدٌ لَّآ إِلَـٰهَ إِلَّا هُوَ الرَّحْمَـٰنُ الرَّحِيمُ

III. Tawheed al-Asmaa' wa-sifaat

And Allāh has the most excellent and perfect Names, so call on Him by them… (al-A'rāf:180)

وَلِلَّهِ الْأَسْمَآءُ الْحُسْنَىٰ فَادْعُوهُ بِهَا

All 3 categories of Tawheed in one ayah

Lord of the heavens and the earth, and all that is between them, so worship Him (alone) and be constant and patient in His worship. Do you know of any who is similar to Him?

(Maryam:65)

رَّبُّ السَّمَاوَاتِ وَالْأَرْضِ وَمَا بَيْنَهُمَا فَاعْبُدْهُ وَاصْطَبِرْ لِعِبَادَتِهِ هَلْ تَعْلَمُ لَهُ سَمِيًّا

Ahādeeth to memorise

Hadeeth 1 – 5 Pillars of Islām

Ibn ‘Umar, the son of ‘Umar bin al-Khattāb ﷺ said: I heard the Messenger of Allāh ﷺ say:

بُنِىَ الْإِسْلَامُ عَلَى خَمْسٍ: شَهَادَةِ أَنْ لَآ إِلَهَ إِلَّا اللهُ وَأَنَّ مُحَمَّدًا رَسُولُ اللهِ، وَإِقَامِ الصَّلَاةِ، وَإِيتَاءِ الزَّكَاةِ،
وَحَجِّ الْبَيْتِ، وَصَوْمِ رَمَضَانَ

“Islām is built upon five (pillars), testifying that none has the right to be worshipped except Allāh alone and that Muhammad ﷺ is the Messenger of Allāh, establishing the (daily) prayers, paying the Zakaat, making the pilgrimage and fasting in Ramadān.”

(Sahīh al-Bukhārī)

Hadeeth 2 – The Right of Allāh

From a long hadeeth, Mu’aadh bin Jabal ﷺ narrated:
The Prophet ﷺ said:

حَقُّ اللهِ عَلَى الْعِبَادِ أَنْ يَعْبُدُوهُ وَلَا يُشْرِكُوا بِهِ شَيْئًا وَحَقُّ الْعِبَادِ عَلَى اللهِ أَنْ لَّا يُعَذِّبَ مَنْ لَّا يُشْرِكُ بِهِ
شَيْئًا

“The Right of Allāh upon His slaves is that they worship Him alone and not to associate anything with Him in worship, and the right of the slaves upon Allāh is not to punish any person who does not associate anything with Him in worship.”

(Sahīh al-Bukhārī & Muslim)

Hadeeth 3 – Tawheed protects from the Hell-Fire

'Itbaan ﵁ narrated that the Prophet ﷺ said:

فَإِنَّ اللهَ قَدْ حَرَّمَ عَلَى النَّارِ مَنْ قَالَ لَا إِلَهَ إِلَّا اللهُ. يَبْتَغِي بِذَلِكَ وَجْهَ اللهِ

"Indeed Allāh has forbidden Hell for the person who testifies: There is nothing worthy of worship in truth except Allāh alone, seeking thereby nothing but Allāh's Face."

(Sahīh al-Bukhārī & Muslim)

Hadeeth 4 – Follow the Sunnah & stay away from what the Prophet ﷺ forbade

Abū Hurairah ﵁ narrated that the Prophet ﷺ said:

مَا نَهَيْتُكُمْ عَنْهُ فَاجْتَنِبُوهُ، وَمَا أَمَرْتُكُمْ بِهِ فَأْتُوا مِنْهُ مَا اسْتَطَعْتُمْ

"What I have prohibited you from, stay well away from it, and what I have ordered you with, do as much of it as you are able."

(Sahīh al-Bukhārī & Muslim)

Hadeeth 5 – Being sincere

Abū Hafs 'Umar bin Al-Khattāb ﵁ said: I heard the Messenger of Allāh ﷺ say:

إِنَّمَا الأَعْمَالُ بِالنِّيَّاتِ، وَإِنَّمَا لِكُلِّ امْرِئٍ مَا نَوَى

"Indeed actions are but by intentions and there is for every person only that which they intended."

(Sahīh al-Bukhārī)

FIQH

Wudhu

&

Salāh

Wudhu (Ablution)

Before a Muslim prays, they must be in a state of Tahārah (purity), because the Prophet ﷺ said:

"No Salāh is accepted without Wudhu."

(Sahīh Muslim)

Therefore, Wudhu is a condition of the Prayer.

We must do Wudhu the way the Prophet ﷺ did so.

Wudhu is:

1. Performed using clean and pure water.
2. Make sure not to waste water.
3. Wash every limb properly leaving no area dry.

Some benefits of Wudhu

1. The Prophet Muhammad ﷺ informed us that our sins are wiped away with every drop of water.
2. The Prophet Muhammad ﷺ will recognise his ummah (nation) on the Day of Judgement by the illumination of the limbs washed in Wudhu.

We should love making Wudhu!

How to make Wudhu according to the Sunnah of the Prophet Muhammad ﷺ.

1. Have the intention to do Wudhu and then say بِسۡمِ ٱللهِ [In the Name of Allāh]

2. Wash your hands from the tip of your fingers up to the wrists and run your fingers on your hand and then run fingers on your left hand.

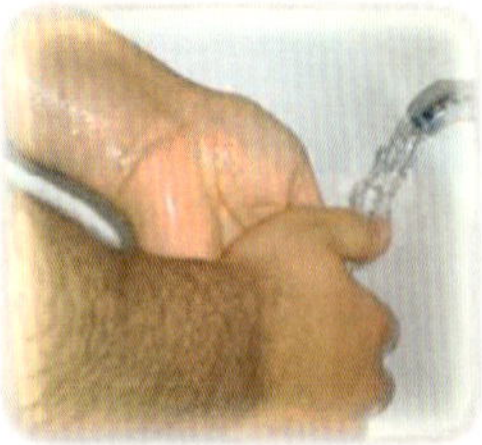

3. Scoop water in your right hand and take into the mouth and nose at the same time, then rinse your **mouth** thoroughly and exhale the water from your nose with your left hand. (up to 3 times)

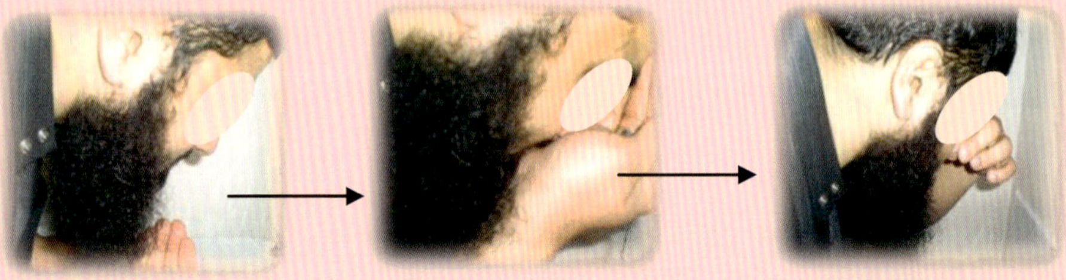

4. Wash your face thoroughly starting from the top of the forehead all the way down to the bottom of the chin, also covering both sides of the face

up to the earlobes. (up to 3 times)

5. Wash your right arm (starting from the tip of the fingers) up to and including the elbow, then repeat this for the left arm. (up to 3 times)

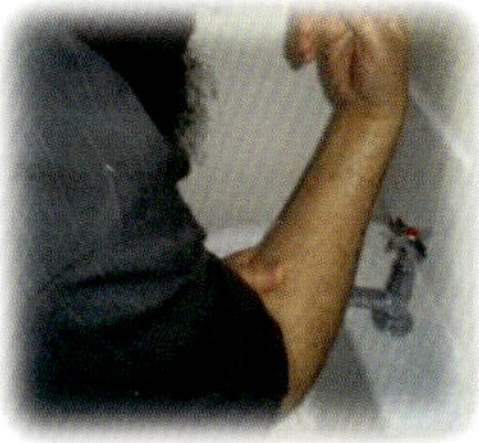

→

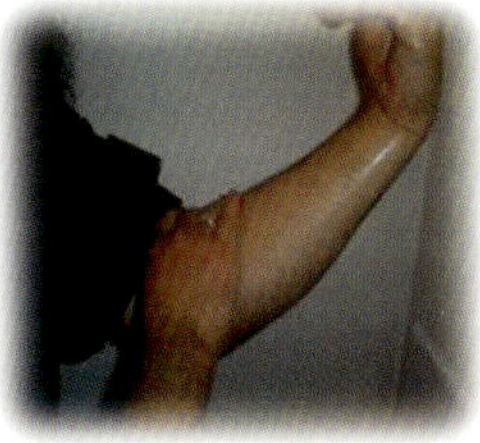

6. Wet your hands again to wipe your head from the front of the head up to the back and then from the back to the front.

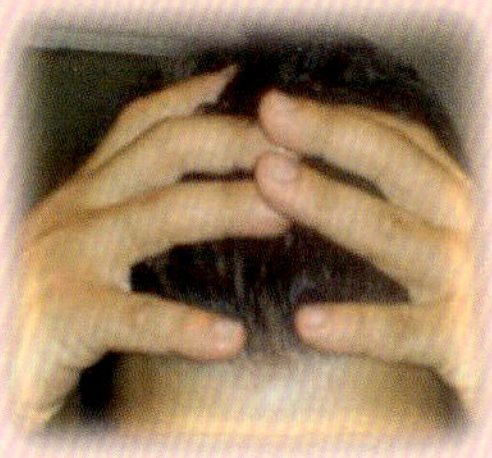

→

7. Using your index fingers wipe both ears from the inside and use the thumbs at the same time to wipe the back of the ears.

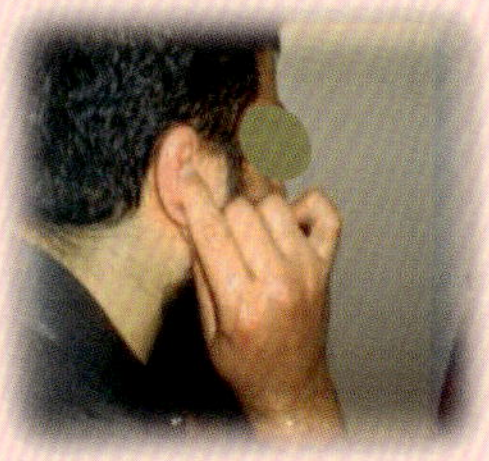

8. Wash your right foot first from the toes up to and including the ankle and run the little finger between the toes, then wash your left foot in the same manner. (up to 3 times)

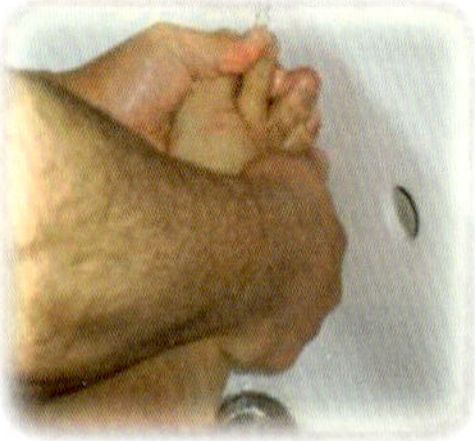 → 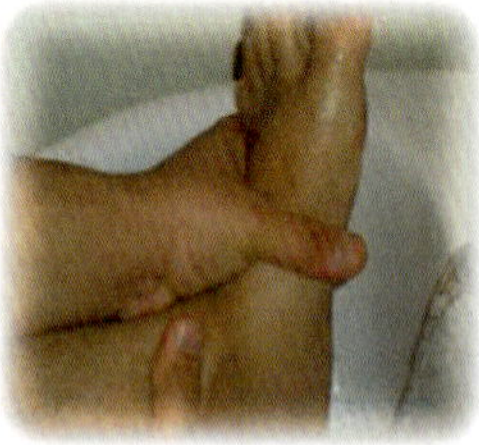

After completing the above actions, say:

أَشْهَدُ أَنْ لَّآ إِلَهَ إِلَّا اللهُ وَحْدَهُ لَا شَرِيكَ لَهُ، وَأَشْهَدُ أَنَّ مُحَمَّداً عَبْدُهُ وَرَسُولُهُ

"I bear witness that none has the right to be worshipped except Allāh alone without any partner. And I bear witness that Muhammad ﷺ is His slave and Messenger."

اللَّهُمَّ اجْعَلْنِي مِنَ التَّوَّابِينَ وَاجْعَلْنِي مِنَ الْمُتَطَهِّرِينَ

"O Allāh, make me from those who turn to You in repentance and make me from those who purify themselves."

(Sahīh Muslim & Tirmidhi:55)

Or:

سُبْحَانَكَ اللَّهُمَّ وَبِحَمْدِكَ، أَشْهَدُ أَنْ لَّآ إِلَهَ إِلَّا أَنْتَ، أَسْتَغْفِرُكَ وَأَتُوبُ إِلَيْكَ

"I declare You free of all imperfections, and all praise is for You. I testify that none has the right to be worshipped but You. I seek Your forgiveness, and I turn in repentance to You."

(Sahīh at-Targheeb:220)

If you have made Wudhu and you put your socks on and then you break your Wudhu whilst still having your socks on, you only need to wipe over the top of your socks and not wash your feet (as shown). This is known as Mas-ah, which can be done for a day from the first wipe.

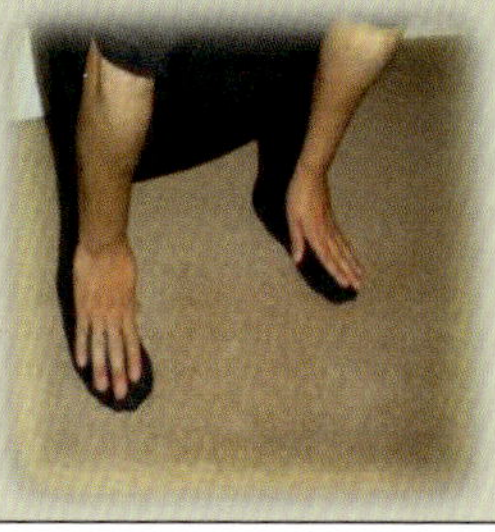

What breaks Wudhu?

1- Defecating, urinating or passing wind.

2- Loss of consciousness due to sleep or other reasons.

3- Eating camel's meat.

Salāh (Prayer)

(Second Pillar of Islām) – The Prophet's Prayer

Definition of Salāh

"Statements and actions which are known, that begin with Takbeer (saying Allāhu Akbar) and end with Tasleem (saying Assalaamu alaykum wa Rahmatullah) with the intention to worship Allāh."

Every Muslim must pray how the Prophet ﷺ prayed and how he taught his noble Companions, as he himself said:

"Pray as you have seen me pray"

(Sahīh al-Bukhārī)

Virtue of Salaāh

The Prophet ﷺ said: "If there was a river at the door of anyone of you and he took a bath in it five times a day, would you notice any dirt on him?", they said, "Not a trace of dirt would be left," The Prophet ﷺ said: "That is the example of the five prayers with which Allāh wipes out evil deeds." (Sahīh al-Bukhārī & Sahīh Muslim)

All Muslim men and women are commanded to pray five times a day from the age they reach puberty. However, to begin with, our Prophet Muhammad ﷺ commanded parents to teach their children the prayer from the age of seven years (seven years according to Islamic calendar), then when they reach ten years of age they are followed by their parents to make sure they have prayed.

In the beginning, Allāh ordered Muhammad ﷺ to tell his people to pray fifty times a day and out of His favour upon us, He reduced it to five prayers a day, but we will still be rewarded for fifty prayers for praying five daily prayers. How kind is Allāh!

Salāh	Rak'ah	Silent/Loud
Fajr	2	Loud
Dhuhr	4	Silent
'Asr	4	Silent
Maghrib	3	Loud
'Ishaa'	4	Loud

One must learn how to pray correctly at the correct times. Fajr, Dhuhr, 'Asr, Maghrib and 'Ishaa' are the five daily prayers.

The Salāh is the second most important pillar of Islām after the Shahadah so we must learn how to perform it correctly according to the way of Prophet Muhammad ﷺ. He prayed in front of his noble Companions for many years until he died and they then taught others how to pray correctly. This is how everything in Islām was learnt by the Companions directly from our beloved Prophet Muhammad ﷺ and then passed on to the next generations, later on, people started writing the very same knowledge so it would not be lost.

Alhamdulillah we see this knowledge preserved in the books as it was taught by our Prophet ﷺ.

One must make Wudhu correctly before praying. If he cannot use water due to being ill or if water is not available then he can pray by performing ***Tayammum***. It is from the mercy of Allāh who made this affair so easy without putting any difficulty upon us.

How to perform Tayammum

I. One should mention the Name of Allāh by saying "Bismillaah".
II. He should strike both hands once on the earth (soil, stone or ground etc) which is clean.
III. Wipe the entire face with your hands.
IV. Wipe the hands with one another.

Important things to remember for the Salāh

I. Allāh made the whole earth a clean place for us where we can pray except for the toilets and the graveyard.

II. Make sure that the place where you pray is clean from any impurity.

III. It is allowed to pray without a prayer mat, our Prophet ﷺ often prayed on the ground without any sheet on it. [**Note:** There should be no pictures of living beings on display. A Muslim should not take pictures of living beings and should not hang them in the houses as the angels do not enter those houses where pictures are displayed.]

IV. Make sure you stand close to a Sutrah. A **Sutrah** (screen/cover) is an object used by a person performing Salāh as a barrier between himself and one passing in front of him. Even if you are praying in the front row, you should be close to the Sutrah. Sutrah could be a wall, pillar, chair or any object that is one forearm in height placed in front of where you prostrate (Sajdah). A Sutrah is used so people do not pass in front of you, if someone still tries to pass through then you should stop them as we were ordered by the Prophet ﷺ.

V. One must wear nice, loose and clean clothing, free from bad odour. Clothes should cover the body fully and not be tightly fitted.

VI. Clothing should have no pictures on them.

VII. Boys must cover their body from the shoulders to below the knees and the clothing should not be below the ankles inside the prayer or outside the prayer as it is a major sin for the men to let their garment drag (be it trousers or their thobe) below the ankles.

VIII. Girls must wear a headscarf and must cover their entire body except their face and hands.

IX. Extra care must be taken when praying in the Masjid as going to the Masjid with dirty clothes and smelling of bad odour harms other people in the Masjid.

X. Our Prophet ﷺ warned us from going to the Masjid if you have eaten onions or garlic due to its bad smell, which is not pleasant for others. So how about praying with clothes or socks which have a bad smell?

XI. When praying, make sure you do not rush. Pray calmly, take your time and rest in each position of the prayer. This is very important because if you rush and do not rest in each position then your prayer is invalid. Remember, you are standing in front of Allāh, the Lord of all of creation.

Conditions of the Salāh

1. Islām
2. Sanity
3. Age of discernment
4. Purification from minor and major impurity
5. Removing impurities from body, clothes and place.
6. Covering the ‘Awrah
7. Prayer time has entered
8. Facing the direction of the Qiblah
9. The Intention

How to pray according to the Sunnah of the Prophet Muhammad ﷺ?

1) Niyyah (Intention)

Niyyah means to plan to do an act. In Islām intention before the Salāh is to plan and be sure in your heart that you are going to offer this specific prayer for the sake of Allāh alone, free from showing off and according to the Sunnah. You must intend what prayer you are going to pray, is it Fajr, Dhuhr or ‘Asr etc and is it an obligatory or Sunnah prayer. Remember, this is done in the heart and not upon the tongue.

The Prophet Muhammad ﷺ did not utter with his tongue which prayer he was going to pray. He ﷺ is our example to follow.

2) Qiyām (Standing)

Qiyām is to stand straight facing the Qiblah, you should keep your feet shoulder width apart whilst facing the Qiblah. It begins with raising both hands (palms facing the Qiblah) to the ears or shoulders (without touching the ears), saying takbeeratul-ihrām (the opening takbeer).

This is to say اللهُ أَكْبَر (Allāh is the Greatest). By saying this takbeer you have entered the prayer and now many things will become prohibited for you which were allowed before the prayer such as talking, eating, drinking, laughing, looking around etc.

Now place your right hand on the back of your left hand and place them on the chest, keep your eyes towards your place of prostration in front of you.

Opening supplication of Qiyām: (This Du'ā should be read in a low voice)

سُبْحَانَكَ اللَّهُمَّ وَبِحَمْدِكَ وَتَبَارَكَ اسْمُكَ وَتَعَالَى جَدُّكَ وَلَآ إِلَهَ غَيْرُكَ

"I declare You free and far removed from all imperfections, O Allāh, and all praise is for You. Blessed is Your Name. Great and Exalted is Your kingdom and none has the right to be worshipped except You."

Once you have read the above Du'ā recite Sūrah al-Fātihah. This is a **must** in all the prayers and if you don't recite this Sūrah then the prayer is invalid. If you are praying Fajr, Maghrib or 'Ishaa' on your own then you should read Sūrah al-Fātihah out loud and if you are praying behind the Imām then you should listen to him quietly. When you pray Dhuhr and 'Asr then one must read this in a low voice whether you are praying on your own or behind the Imām.

I seek refuge with Allāh from the Shaytaan, the rejected one.	أعوذُ بِاللهِ مِنَ الشَّيْطٰنِ الرَّجِيمِ
In the Name of Allāh, the Most-Merciful, the Bestower of Mercy.	بِسْمِ اللهِ الرَّحْمٰنِ الرَّحِيمِ
All praise is for Allāh, the Lord of all creation.	الْحَمْدُ لِلّٰهِ رَبِّ الْعَالَمِينَ
The Most Merciful, the Bestower of Mercy.	الرَّحْمٰنِ الرَّحِيمِ
The Only Owner (and the Only Ruling Judge) of the Day of Recompense (i.e. the Day of Resurrection).	مَالِكِ يَوْمِ الدِّينِ
You (alone) we worship, and You (alone) we ask for help (for each and everything).	إِيَّاكَ نَعْبُدُ وَإِيَّاكَ نَسْتَعِينُ
Guide us to the Straight Way.	اهدِنَــا الصِّرَاطَ الْمُسْتَقِيمَ
The Way of those on whom You have bestowed Your Grace, not (the way) of those who earned Your Anger, nor of those who went astray.	صِرَاطَ الَّذِينَ أَنْعَمْتَ عَلَيْهِمْ غَيْرِ الْمَغْضُوبِ عَلَيْهِمْ وَلَا الضَّالِّينَ

Then say aloud with the Imām آمـين (may Allāh accept it) or in a low voice if you are praying a silent prayer. After reciting Sūrah al-Fātihah recite another Sūrah from the Qur'ān.

3) Rukoo' (Bowing)

Now raise your hands to your shoulder or ears (this is known as Rafa'a al-Yadayn) and say الله أكبر (Allāh is the Greatest) and then go down for Rukoo'. Bend at the hips, place the hands firmly upon the knees (as shown in the picture), he should spread his fingers, as if he were grasping his knees. Keep the back and head straight in line with each other and look at the place of Sujood.

Rest in this position and say the following Du'ā three times or more.

Supplication of Rukoo':

سُبْحَانَ رَبِّيَ الْعَظِيمِ

"I declare my Lord, the Supreme, free and far removed from all imperfections."

4) I'tidaal (standing after Rukoo')

Then rise up back from Rukoo' raising the hands to the ears or shoulders and then place your hands to the side and say the following Du'ā.

Supplication for Qiyām after Rukoo':

سَمِعَ اللهُ لِمَنْ حَمِدَهُ

"Allāh listens and responds to the one who praises Him."

رَبَّنَا وَلَكَ الْحَمْدُ

"O our Lord! And all praise is for You."

Direct your head and eyes to the place of Sajdah and make sure you stand straight until every part of the body returns to its place.

5) Sajdah (Prostration)

Say اللهُ أَكْبَرُ and go down for Sajdah.

I. When going down put your hands on the ground first (as shown in the picture), then your knees, followed by the forehead and nose, now you are in Sujood.

II. Make sure your arms do not touch your sides and your elbows do not touch the ground.

III. Your heels should be joined together, toes facing the Qiblah, fingers should be joined together facing the Qiblah and your knees should not touch your stomach.

IV. Whilst in Sujood, seven body parts must be touching the ground and not one of them should be off the ground until you sit up from Sujood. These seven body parts are the nose & forehead, palms of both hands, both knees and the toes of both feet.

V. Rest in this position and say the following Du'ā three times or more.

سُبْحَانَ رَبِّيَ الأَعْلَى

"I declare my Lord, the Most High, free and far removed from all imperfections."

6) Jalsah

Say اللهُ أَكْبَرُ and sit up, sit on your left foot with your right foot vertical to the ground and your toes pointing in the direction of the Qiblah. Sit relaxed with your back straight and your hands on your lower thighs close to your knees.

Supplication of Jalsah:

رَبِّ اغْفِرْ لِي، رَبِّ اغْفِرْ لِي

"O My Lord forgive me! O My Lord forgive me!"

7) Second Sajdah

Say اللهُ أَكْبَرُ and prostrate a second time as you did before in step 5.

8) Jalsatul-Istiraahah

Say اللهُ أَكْبَرُ and sit up again as before for a moment (known as Jalsatul-Istiraahah) until you are settled. There is no Du'ā in this sitting. Then make fists with both hands to support yourself back to the standing position as was in the beginning.

This completes one Rak'ah (unit) of prayer.

9) Second Rak'ah

Repeat the prayer performed as in steps 2 to 7 (from Sūrah al-Fātihah up to the second Sajdah)

10) Tashahhud

This time when you sit up after step 9, you will stay in the sitting position relaxed with your back straight.

I. Keep your left hand on your left thigh, make a fist with your right hand, and point with your index finger in the direction of the Qiblah.
II. With the middle finger and the thumb form a circle.
III. Keep your eyes on the index finger as you recite.

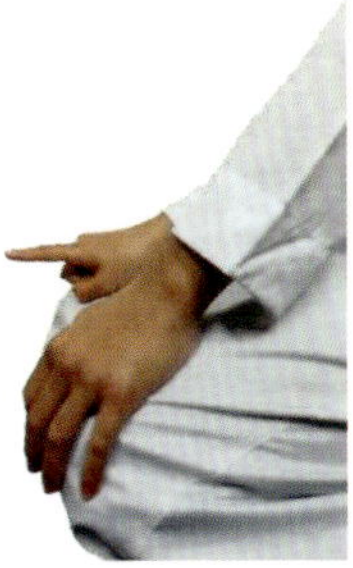

Supplication of Tashahhud:

التَّحِيَّاتُ لِلَّهِ وَالصَّلَوَاتُ وَالطَّيِّبَاتُ، السَّلَامُ عَلَى النَّبِيِّ وَرَحْمَةُ اللهِ وَبَرَكَاتُهُ،

السَّلَامُ عَلَيْنَا وَعَلَى عِبَادِ اللهِ الصَّالِحِيْنَ،

"Words of praise and glorification are for Allāh alone and prayers, worship and pure words also. May Allāh send peace and security upon the Prophet and His Mercy and blessings. May Allāh send peace and security upon us and upon all of His righteous servants."

أَشْهَدُ أَنْ لَّآ إِلَهَ إِلَّا اللهُ وَأَشْهَدُ أَنَّ مُحَمَّدًا عَبْدُهُ وَرَسُولُهُ

"I bear witness that none has the right to be worshipped except Allāh and I bear witness that Muhammad is His slave and His Messenger."

Sending the Prayers on Prophet Muhammad ﷺ:

اللَّهُمَّ صَلِّ عَلَى مُحَمَّدٍ وَعَلَى آلِ مُحَمَّدٍ كَمَا صَلَّيْتَ عَلَى إِبْرَاهِيمَ وَعَلَى آلِ إِبْرَاهِيمَ إِنَّكَ حَمِيدٌ مَجِيدٌ

"O Allāh! Send Your prayers (honour) on Muhammad and the true followers of Muhammad, just as you sent your prayers (honour) on Ibrāhīm and the righteous offspring of Ibrāhīm, Indeed, You are deserving of all praise, perfect in glory and honour."

اللَّهُمَّ بَارِكْ عَلَى مُحَمَّدٍ وَعَلَى آلِ مُحَمَّدٍ كَمَا بَارَكْتَ عَلَى إِبْرَاهِيمَ وَعَلَى آلِ إِبْرَاهِيمَ إِنَّكَ حَمِيدٌ مَجِيدٌ

"O Allāh! Send Your blessings on Muhammad and the true followers of Muhammad, just as you sent your Blessings on Ibrāhīm and the righteous offspring of Ibrāhīm, Indeed, You are deserving of all praise, perfect in glory and honour."

The closing supplications:

اللَّهُمَّ إِنِّي أَعُوذُ بِكَ مِنْ عَذَابِ جَهَنَّمَ وَمِنْ عَذَابِ القَبْرِ وَمِنْ فِتْنَةِ المَحْيَا وَالمَمَاتِ وَمِنْ شَرِّ فِتْنَةِ المَسِيحِ الدَّجَّالِ

"O Allāh, I seek refuge with You from the punishment of the Hell-Fire and from the punishment of the grave and from the trials of life and death and from the tribulation of the Dajjaal (false Messiah)."

11) Tasleem

End the prayer with tasleem, turn your head towards the **right** shoulder and then towards the **left** shoulder and say the following Du'ā each time.

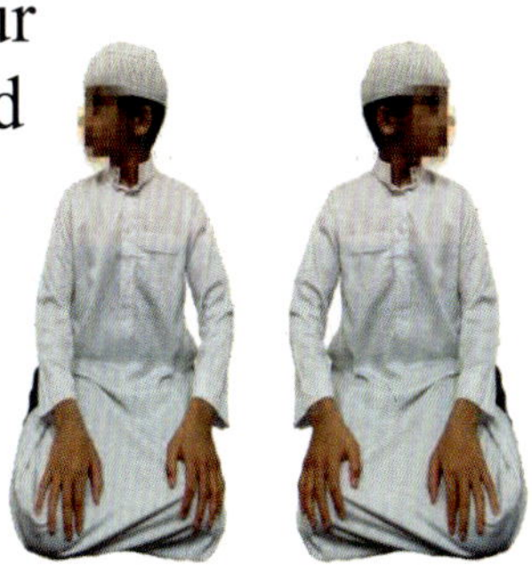

The supplications of tasleem:

السَّلامُ عَلَيْكُمْ وَرَحْمَةُ الله

"May Allāh's peace and security be upon you, and His Mercy."

السَّلامُ عَلَيْكُمْ وَرَحْمَةُ الله

"May Allāh's peace and security be upon you, and His Mercy."

The above is how you pray two Rak'ah of prayer.

(Two Rak'ah are prayed for fajr and Sunnah prayers. We will learn when and what Sunnah prayers are to be prayed in the next level inshaa-Allāh.

If you are praying a **three** or **four** Rak'ah prayer then on the last tashahhud sit as you see in the picture below. (Sit on your left buttock by bringing your left foot under your right leg.)

Pillars of the Prayer are Fourteen:

1. Qiyām (If you're able)
2. Takbeeratul-ihrām (opening Takbir – Allāhu Akbar)
3. Recitation of al-Fātihah
4. Rukoo’
5. Standing after Rukoo’ (bowing)
6. Sujood (upon seven limbs: forehead with nose, two palms, two feet, two knees)
7. Rising up from Sujood
8. Sitting between the two Sujood
9. Last Tashahhud
10. Sitting for Tashahhud
11. Sending the Prayers upon the Prophet ﷺ
12. Tasleem (saying As-salamu alaykum warahmatullah)
13. Having tranquillity in all the pillars
14. Tarteeb (following the order)

The First

&

The Last Prophet

The First Prophet

Ādam عليه السلام

There are many stories of the Prophets mentioned in the Qur'ān. Allāh did not just mention them to make it interesting for the reader, rather we learn Islām through them.

Furthermore, we take lessons from the nations that disobeyed their Prophets who were sent by Allāh to teach them Tawheed. Allāh punished these nations for not worshipping Him alone.

Ādam عليه السلام was the first of mankind and was the first of the Prophets. There are many benefits for us in the story of the creation of Ādam and Hawa.

When Allāh created Ādam عليه السلام in Jannah, He left his body in Jannah for a period of time without the soul. Iblees (Satan) would come to look at the body and go around it and then leave as he was jealous of Ādam عليه السلام.

How Ādam عليه السلام was created and when was the soul blown into him? The Prophet Muhammad ﷺ told us about this incident in the authentic narrations.

The Prophet Muhammad ﷺ informed us that Allāh created:

- The earth on Saturday
- The mountains on Sunday
- The trees on Monday
- That which is disliked on Tuesday
- Light on Wednesday
- Animals on Thursday
- And then He created Ādam عليه السلام between 'Asr and Maghrib on Friday (Sahīh Muslim)

In another hadeeth, he stated that when the soul was blown into Ādam's عليه السلام body by Allāh, it moved around his body and then it reached his head at which point Ādam sneezed. After sneezing, he said, "Alhamdulillah" and Allāh said, "YarhamukAllāh" (may Allāh show you mercy). (as-Saheehah: 2159)

Allāh informed us in the Qur'ān that the humans are from the offspring of Prophet Ādam عليه السلام.

يَٰٓأَيُّهَا ٱلنَّاسُ ٱتَّقُوا۟ رَبَّكُمُ ٱلَّذِى خَلَقَكُم مِّن نَّفْسٍ وَٰحِدَةٍ وَخَلَقَ مِنْهَا زَوْجَهَا وَبَثَّ مِنْهُمَا رِجَالًا كَثِيرًا وَنِسَآءً

"O mankind! Be dutiful to your Lord, Who created you from a single person (Ādam), and from him (Ādam) He created his wife [Hawa (Eve)], and from them both He created many men and women." (an-Nisā':1)

The Prophet ﷺ said that when Allāh created Ādam, He wiped his back and all of mankind (upto the Day of Judgement) came from his back by way of this wiping. He touched Ādam's right shoulder and all of his offspring destined for Jannah came about. Then He struck Ādam's left shoulder and all of his offspring destined for the Hell-Fire came about.

Allāh created Ādam عليه السلام upon the best form. When Allāh created him, He ordered the angels and Iblees to prostrate to Ādam عليه السلام. All the angels obeyed the order of Allāh and prostrated to Ādam. However, Iblees, the Shaytān did not obey Allāh and he made a false comparison that Allāh created him from fire and He created Ādam from clay, hence he said, "I am better than Ādam and so will not prostrate to him."

قَالَ مَا مَنَعَكَ أَلَّا تَسْجُدَ إِذْ أَمَرْتُكَ ۖ قَالَ أَنَا خَيْرٌ مِّنْهُ خَلَقْتَنِي مِن نَّارٍ وَخَلَقْتَهُ مِن طِينٍ

(Allāh) said, "What prevented you (O Iblees) that you did not prostrate yourself when I commanded you?" Iblees said, "I am better than him (Ādam), You created me from fire and him You created him from clay." (al-A'raaf:12)

Allāh became angry at Iblees due to him being filled with pride and arrogance and this led him to become a disbeliever.

Even if we look at this false comparison of Iblees, then one will see that the clay or soil in reality has many benefits. For example, it produces vegetation and fruits, it is gentle in its nature and brings about many benefits, as opposed to the fire which is hot and burns things and it is destructive as Allāh uses the fire to punish. When moulding clay it takes time and needs care whereas fire comes about in an instance.

Some facts about Ādam عليه السلام & Hawa

1. Allāh taught Ādam the names of all things.
2. He taught him the nature of everything.
3. He spoke to him.
4. He sent Ādam to the angels and commanded him to say Salām to all the angels, so the angels responded to him with "**Wa Alaykum as-Salaam wa-Rahmatullaahi wa-Barakaatuhu**".
5. There were 10 generations between Ādam عليه السلام and Nuh (Noah) عليه السلام.
6. Allāh commanded Ādam عليه السلام and his wife Hawa to eat from wherever they wanted in Jannah but ordered them not to go near a specific tree and to not eat from it. It is not known to us what tree or fruit it was.
7. Shaytān tricked them to eat from this tree, he said to Hawa that if you eat from this tree then you will become eternal and will live in Jannah forever.
8. Hawa convinced Ādam to eat from the tree. Upon eating its' fruit, they became naked.

9. Allāh expelled them both from Jannah. They both regretted and turned back to Allāh. Allāh taught them how to ask for forgiveness.

قَالَا رَبَّنَا ظَلَمْنَآ أَنفُسَنَا وَإِن لَّمْ تَغْفِرْ لَنَا وَتَرْحَمْنَا لَنَكُونَنَّ مِنَ الْخَاسِرِينَ

They said: "Our Lord! We have wronged ourselves. If You do not forgive us and do not bestow upon us Your Mercy, we shall certainly be of the losers." (al-A'rāf:23)

There are verses in the Qur'ān mentioning their supplication to Allāh for forgiveness, so Allāh forgave them. This was just one act of disobedience and due to this they were expelled from Jannah. Imagine how much mankind sin and disobey their Lord, day and night. Yet Ādam عليه السلام regretted and turned back to Allāh in repentance and sought His forgiveness.

Allāh decreed 1,000 years of life for Ādam عليه السلام. When Allāh created the children of Ādam from Ādam's back, Ādam عليه السلام saw a man with light between his eyes. Ādam عليه السلام asked who is this? It was said to him that this was Dāwūd عليه السلام (Allāh's Prophet and Messenger) who would live for a certain number of years. Ādam عليه السلام asked Allāh to grant 40 years from his life to Dāwūd عليه السلام and so Ādam عليه السلام lived for 960 years.

The Last Prophet

Muhammad ﷺ

Before the coming of Prophet Muhammad ﷺ, the Arabs used to worship idols, which they made with their own hands, how strange!

How can you worship that which is created, that does not speak nor hear? What kind of god is this?!

Some used to make the idols out of dates. When they went on a journey, they would take this idol with them and when they became hungry, they would eat the idol!

There were also Jews and Christians among the Arabs, but they had changed that which was brought to them by their Prophets and they also worshipped the creation, for example the Christians worshipped Prophet 'Isa عليه السلام and the Jews worshipped Prophet 'Uzayr عليه السلام.

The Arabs used to bury their daughters alive because they considered it to be a shame to have a daughter, what an evil belief!

They used to drink alcohol, gamble, treat their women badly, the weak and the poor were oppressed.

Arabs used to live in tribes, they often used to fight with other tribes over small issues. These feuds would often lead to war and were carried on through generations.

Imagine how much ignorance they lived in. For this reason, there was a need for a Prophet of Allāh to be sent to them, to take them out of the darkness of worshipping created things into the light of worshipping the Creator, the One Who created them, provided for them and to Whom they shall return.

Out of Allāh's Mercy and Kindness, He revealed the Qur'ān to Prophet Muhammad ﷺ as a guide:

1. To that which is pleasing to Allāh, from the various types of worship.
2. How to interact with one another.
3. To establish justice amongst the people, giving everyone their due right regardless of their colour and tribe.

Prophet Muhammad ﷺ

1. Was born in Makkah in Arabia.
2. To a noble Arab tribe called Quraysh.
3. His father was 'Abdullah son of 'Abdul Muttalib, who died just before Muhammad ﷺ was born.
4. His mother was Āminah.
5. The good news of his birth was sent to his grandfather 'Abdul Muttalib who was overjoyed and named him Muhammad (ﷺ).

6. He was from the descendents of Prophet Ibrāhīm عليه السلام.
7. Soon after he was born, he was sent to a foster mother, Halimah, to live in the desert. Life in the desert was good for the babies as there was fresh air, water and plenty of space for them to run around and play.

One day, out in the desert where Muhammad ﷺ and other children were playing, an angel was sent by Allāh to purify Muhammad ﷺ. Halimah's children became frightened and ran home to tell their mother of what had happened. Halimah decided to send Muhammad ﷺ back to his mother. He lived in the desert for six years and when he returned to his mother, she was very happy to have him back. Later, his mother took him to the city of Madinah and on the way back she died. Muhammad ﷺ was taken and cared for by his grandfather in Makkah. He was only eight years old when his grandfather died, his uncle Abū Tālib, happily took him into his care.

People in Makkah believed that Allāh was their Lord but they did not worship Allāh alone. Rather, they would go around the K'abah where there were many idols made of wood and stones which they would worship. Muhammad ﷺ knew these idols could not help or protect anyone.

Muhammad ﷺ being a young boy would look after the sheep in the mountains. When he reached the age of twelve, his uncle Abū Tālib began taking him on trade journeys to Ash-Shām (present day Syria, Jordan and Palestine). He was known as al-Saadiq and al-Ameen (truthful and trustworthy) by the people in and around Makkah.

A noble woman called Khadījah ﵂ heard about the noble character of Muhammad ﷺ and was informed by many of his truthfulness, so she requested from him to sell her goods in Ash-Shām.

Muhammad ﷺ accepted Khadījah's ﵂ proposal of work and set out on the journey to Ash-Shām. When Muhammad ﷺ returned, Khadījah ﵂ found that her profits were more than she had ever seen before which pleased her very much, but more than that, it was the noble character of Muhammad ﷺ that pleased her.

Khadījah ﵂ was an intelligent and noble woman and so when she heard and observed this from Muhammad ﷺ, she sent a message to him requesting to marry him.

Muhammad ﷺ informed his uncles of her request and they agreed to his marriage with Khadījah ﵂ and he was twenty-five years old. Muhammad's ﷺ uncle, Hamzah ﵁ went to the house of Khadījah's ﵂ father and made the proposal of marriage.

They were happily married and had four daughters and two sons. His two sons died while they were very young.

Muhammad ﷺ would often go out in the mountains and stay in the cave called Hira, where he would remember Allāh and think about His blessings. One day when he was in deep thought in the very same cave, an angel called Jibrā'īl عليه السلام came down from the heavens with a message from Allāh.

Jibrā'īl عليه السلام said to him, "Read!"

Muhammad ﷺ replied, "I cannot read". Jibrā'īl عليه السلام pressed and squeezed Muhammad ﷺ asking him to read again. Muhammad ﷺ replied, "I cannot read". This time Jibrā'īl عليه السلام pressed and squeezed him harder and said, "Read in the Name of your Lord, who has created everything." Muhammad ﷺ who could not read or write, repeated the words after the angel Jibrā'īl عليه السلام, with the help of Allāh.

It was so scary that he ran home to his wife Khadījah رضي الله عنها and said to her "cover me! cover me!" She asked him what had happened, so he told her what had happened in the cave. Khadījah رضي الله عنها believed his story without a doubt and said to him that Allāh would never disgrace him, for he was a good man who helped the needy and poor, and he was kind to his guests and kept ties of kinship.

Khadījah ﷺ took Muhammad ﷺ and went to see her cousin Warqah bin Nawfal, a blind man who had knowledge of the previous Books that were sent down by Allāh, but were changed and corrupted by the people. He asked Muhammad ﷺ to tell him all that happened to him in the cave. Upon hearing Muhammad's ﷺ story, he replied that the angel Jibrā'īl عليه السلام was the same angel that was sent by Allāh to the Prophet Mūsa عليه السلام. Warqah, the blind man, said to Muhammad ﷺ, "I wish that I was younger or live until the day your people would drive you out of Makkah so I could help you." As this happened to other Prophets who came before.

Not long after this meeting, Warqah died and the angel Jibrā'īl عليه السلام did not come for some time.

Prophet Muhammad ﷺ began to call people to Islām. Khadījah رضي الله عنها was the first to accept Islām, after that Muhammad's ﷺ freed slave, Zaid, his best friend Abū Bakr and his cousin 'Ali, all accepted Islām.

Anyone who obeys Allāh and follows His Messenger Muhammad ﷺ is called a Muslim.

At the beginning Muhammad ﷺ called people to Islām secretly and would teach them Islām in a house owned by Al-Arqam. He warned people from worshipping idols. The message of Muhammad ﷺ was a simple message, which was to give **all** your worship to the One Lord Who brought everything into existence.

The people knew the Prophet Muhammad ﷺ not to be a liar and that he was trustworthy, but many were not willing to accept the message he came with. They did not want to change their way of life.

So the leaders of the Quraysh began to spread lies about the Prophet ﷺ, they did this to stop the people believing and following the message he came with.

Even though the Prophet Muhammad ﷺ faced many harms, either by way of people calling him bad names or trying to hurt him physically, he continued to call the people to worship Allāh alone with good manners and patience.

Some of the people who accepted the message were tortured and killed by the Quraysh.

Why were they killed or physically hurt? For no other reason except for believing that Allāh is their Lord and the only One Who is deserving of their worship.

Soon many people started to enter Islām, some by way of hearing the Qur'ān and some by just looking at the Prophet ﷺ and the way he treated others with justice and kindness. The leaders of the Quraysh tried different ways to stop the spread of Islām, they even offered to make the Prophet Muhammad ﷺ the richest person in order to give up his call but he refused. This shows the truthfulness and sincerity of the Prophet Muhammad ﷺ, as he had no concern or care for the worldly matters. No matter how much money a person may have it will not bring them true happiness if they do not follow the religion of Islām.

Allāh has promised those who truly believe and do righteous actions that they will have a happy life and as for those who do not believe and carry out bad actions they will have a sad life. The Prophet ﷺ had no concern for money or leadership, his only concern was to call the people away from the darkness of worshipping created things such as idols, trees, humans etc into the light of worshipping the Creator of everything that exists and to establish justice amongst the people.

When the leaders of Quraysh realised that there was no stopping the call and spread of Islām, they started to kill some of the Muslims and harm them. We should remember the blessing we have, that we live in safety and security and also remember the struggles of the early Muslims (Sahaabah), who strove and sacrificed in order for Allāh's religion to be spread and today it has reached us.

When the Prophet ﷺ saw the harm and difficulties the Muslims were facing, he ordered a group of them to go to Ethiopia, where there was a king who did not oppress the people. The king treated the Muslims kindly and allowed them to stay in his country. Some of the idol worshippers from the Quraysh tried to tell the king to not allow these people to stay in his country and told many lies against the Muslims. However, the king did not listen to their lies as he knew the Muslims were good people. This king later became a Muslim, he was called Najāshi, may Allāh have mercy upon him for treating the Muslims so kindly, those who had been treated badly by the Quraysh.

Back in Makkah, the message of Islām was getting stronger and Islām was spreading outside of Makkah. Ten years after becoming a Prophet, Muhammad's ﷺ wife Khadījah رضي الله عنها and uncle Abū Tālib passed away. This year was known as the year of sorrow. Even with this sadness the Prophet ﷺ still continued in calling the people to the religion of Islām. In this, is a lesson for all of us, we will face times of difficulty in our lives but we should remain patient and hope for the reward of Allāh and never lose hope because this life is only a temporary life, whereas the Hereafter for the believers is everlasting and full of happiness.

Later, the Prophet Muhammad ﷺ went to the city of Tā'if to call the people to worship Allāh alone. He was received with much abuse by the people and they forced him out of the city by throwing stones at him causing him to bleed.

Allāh sent angel Jibrā'īl عليه السلام to the Prophet ﷺ and the angel Jibrā'īl عليه السلام asked the Prophet ﷺ that if he wished, an angel is ready to crush the city for the harm they have caused the Prophet ﷺ.

The Prophet Muhammad ﷺ refused, and made Du'ā to Allāh that their children become Muslims. Look and reflect over the mercy of our Prophet Muhammad ﷺ, even though the people had harmed him, he still wanted good for them and wanted them to be guided, this is how we should be as Muslims, wanting good and guidance for the people and not bringing any harm to the people.

Why do you think Allāh sent **124,000** Prophets and revealed Books to certain Messengers?

It was for none other than the guidance for mankind. **How Great is Allāh's Mercy!**

Family of Prophet Muhammad ﷺ

Now we will learn the names of some of the family of the Prophet Muhammad ﷺ. We must remember that guidance is from Allāh, there were some members of his family who were not Muslim. He ﷺ did not have any brothers or sisters.

‘Abdullah (Father)	Āminah (Mother)
‘Abdul-Muttalib (Grandfather)	Abū Tālib (Paternal uncle)
‘Abbās رضي الله عنه (Paternal uncle)	‘Ali رضي الله عنه (Cousin & Son in-law)
Hamzah رضي الله عنه (Paternal uncle)	Abū Lahab (Paternal uncle)

The noble and pure wives of the Prophet Muhammad ﷺ have been described by Allāh in the Qur’ān as being the Mothers of the Believers.

The Wives of the Prophet Muhammad ﷺ (May Allāh be pleased with them all)	
Khadījah bint Khuwaylid	Zaynab bint Khuzaymah
‘Ā’ishah bint Abi Bakr	Hafsah bint ‘Umar
Ramlah bint Abi Sufyān	Sawdah bint Zam’a
Safiyyah bint Huyayy	Maymunah bint al-Hārith

Juwayriyyah bint al-Haarith	Zaynab bint Jahsh

Hind bint Abi Umayyah

Daughters of the Prophet Muhammad ﷺ (May Allāh be pleased with them all)			
Fātimah	Ruqayyah	Zaynab	Umm Kulthūm

Sons of the Prophet Muhammad ﷺ (May Allāh be pleased with them all)		
Qāsim	Ibrāhīm	‘Abdullah

Grandchildren of the Prophet Muhammad ﷺ (May Allāh be pleased with them all)		
‘Umāmah	Hasan	Hussain

'Asharah Mubasharah

(The 10 given glad tidings of Paradise)

Sahābi is the Arabic word for Companion. A Companion is someone who met Prophet Muhammad ﷺ in his lifetime whilst being a Muslim and died upon Islām. They were specifically chosen by Allāh. They accompanied our Prophet ﷺ and learnt Islām from him directly and spread Islām to others.

There were over one hundred thousand Companions, they were all pious and the best of all the people of Islām. They were pleased with Allāh and Allāh is pleased with them all. Prophet Muhammad ﷺ mentioned many of his Companions by their names specifically that they will be in Paradise. We will learn the names of ten Companions who were given the glad tidings of Paradise in their lifetime by the Prophet Muhammad ﷺ and they are the best of all the Companions.

We use the term "Radhi Allāhu 'anhu" with their names, which means, "may Allāh be pleased with him" for a male Companion and "Radhi Allāhu anha" which means, "may Allāh be pleased with her" for a female Companion.

1. Abū Bakr as-Siddeeq ﵁
2. ‘Umar bin al-Khattāb ﵁
3. ‘Uthmān bin ‘Affān ﵁
4. ‘Ali bin Abi Tālib ﵁
5. Talhah bin ‘Ubaidullah ﵁
6. Az-Zubair bin al-‘Awwām ﵁
7. ‘Abdur-Rahmān bin ‘Awf ﵁
8. Sa’d bin Abi Waqqās ﵁
9. Sa’eed bin Zaid ﵁
10. Abū ‘Ubaidah bin al-Jarrah ﵁

Can you write 10 more names of the noble Companions.

Etiquettes

&

Manners

Basmallah

Prophet Muhammad ﷺ taught us to say بِسۡمِ اللهِ when we want to do certain things. Allāh will help us in that matter and bless it for us.

It is the Sunnah of our beloved Prophet Muhammad ﷺ to say بِسۡمِ اللهِ:

- Before making Wudhu
- Before drinking water
- Before eating food
- Upon entering the house
- Upon entering the Masjid
- Before sleeping
- Before removing our clothes
- When boarding a form of transport (car, train, plane, bicycle etc)

Masjid (Mosque)

The Arabic word for mosque is Masjid. A Masjid is a place in which Muslims pray five times a day. Masaajid (plural of Masjid) are for the worship of Allāh alone. The Masjid plays an important role in the lives of the Muslims. The most beloved of places on the earth to Allāh are the Masaajid. It is a place where the prayer takes place, also where the Qur'ān is taught and read. It is the place where Allāh is mentioned much. It is the place where the knowledge of the religion is taught.

It is where all Muslims no matter what colour they are or where they are from stand together to worship Allāh. It is where the Muslims gather to open their fast in the month of Ramadān.

When it is time for the prayer, the Mu'adhin (the caller to prayer) calls out the Adhān (call to prayer) from the Masjid. When you hear the Adhān, one should say as the Mu'adhin says and you should prepare yourself for the Prayer. The Iqāmah (final call to prayer) is then called by the Mu'adhin just before the prayer, in order to begin the Fardh (obligatory) prayer. Upon hearing the Iqāmah, join the congregation, stand facing the Qiblah, join the feet and shoulders with the person next to you and straighten the rows.

The Imām leads the people in prayer. One must follow the Imām during the prayer. Therefore, when he goes into Rukoo', you follow, when he rises from Rukoo', you rise, when he performs Sajdah, you follow.

It is NOT allowed to go before the Imām in any position of the prayer. This will nullify your prayer.

A prayer which is prayed in congregation in the Masjid is multiplied 27 times to whatever Allāh wills. You should enter the Masjid with your right foot first and leave with the left foot first.

We must keep the Masjid clean at all times. We must not raise our voices in the Masjid.

Du'ā for entering the Masjid

بِسْمِ اللهِ، وَالصَّلَاةُ وَالسَّلَامُ عَلَى رَسُولِ اللهِ، اللَّهُمَّ افْتَحْ لِي أَبْوَابَ رَحْمَتِكَ

In the Name of Allāh and prayers and peace be upon the Messenger of Allāh. O Allāh, open the gates of Your mercy for me.

Du'ā for leaving the Masjid:

بِسْمِ اللهِ وَالصَّلَاةُ وَالسَّلَامُ عَلَى رَسُولِ اللهِ، اللَّهُمَّ إِنِّي أَسْأَلُكَ مِنْ فَضْلِكَ

"In the Name of Allāh and prayers and peace be upon the Messenger of Allāh. O Allāh, I ask You from Your favour and bounties."

Some of the virtues of the Masjid

The Masjid is where much good takes place.

- It is the place where Muslims gather daily for the obligatory prayers.
- It is the place where the Qur'ān is taught and recited.
- It is the place where Islām is taught and learnt.

1. Praying in congregation in the Masjid is twenty-seven times better than praying alone. (Sahīh al- Bukhārī)
2. When you make Wudhu from home and come to the Masjid, for every step you take a sin is removed and you are raised a level (with Allāh). (Sahīh Muslim)
3. When you are coming to the Masjid for the prayer it is as if you are in the prayer, therefore we should speak good when coming to the Masjid.
4. When we finish the prayer in congregation and say the remembrances after the prayer, the angels pray for us.
5. Whoever goes to the Masjid to LEARN good or to teach it then they will have a reward as if they completed the Hajj. (Sahīh at-Targheeb wat-Tarheeb no.86)

Kindness to Parents

After being obedient to Allāh and His Messenger ﷺ, a Muslim must be obedient to his parents. Allāh commanded us to be kind and dutiful to our parents.

وَقَضَىٰ رَبُّكَ أَلَّا تَعْبُدُوٓا۟ إِلَّآ إِيَّاهُ وَبِٱلْوَٰلِدَيْنِ إِحْسَٰنًا ۚ إِمَّا يَبْلُغَنَّ عِندَكَ ٱلْكِبَرَ أَحَدُهُمَآ أَوْ كِلَاهُمَا فَلَا

تَقُل لَّهُمَآ أُفٍّ وَلَا تَنْهَرْهُمَا وَقُل لَّهُمَا قَوْلًا كَرِيمًا

And your Lord has decreed that you worship none but Him. And that you be dutiful to your parents. If one of them or both of them attain old age in your life, say not to them a word of disrespect, nor shout at them but address them with terms of honour.

(al-Israa:23)

Our mothers who carried us with care in their bellies for a long period of time, then gave birth to us followed by raising us, staying up during the night when we were ill.

She raised us with hardship upon hardship, which is why in Islām she has a very high status.

Our fathers who work hard whether it's day or night, hot or cold are always making sure they are earning enough to provide food, clothing and fulfil our needs. He protects his family from any harm.

'Abdullah bin Mas'oud (may Allāh be pleased with him) was a famous Companion, was known to hasten to do good deeds. He once came to Prophet Muhammad ﷺ and asked him, "What action is most beloved to Allāh?" So Prophet Muhammad ﷺ replied, "To offer the prayer at its prescribed time." 'Abdullah bin Mas'oud (may Allāh be pleased with him) asked again and "What after that?" He ﷺ replied, "To be good and dutiful to your parents." (Sahīh al-Bukhārī)

We should talk to our parents with gentleness and be polite. Be respectful and always be helpful to them. We must not talk to them in such a manner which may hurt their feelings or which make them upset.

You must listen to your parents attentively and fulfil whatever they ask you to do. Our Prophet ﷺ emphasised that we must be very kind to our parents and do not speak to them with bad manners. If you are kind to your parents then they will be very happy with you and will love you more. If your parents are happy with you, then Allāh will be happy with you.

You should smile at your parents, give them Salām when you see them and kiss them on their head whenever you come home or they come home. You will see that it will make them very happy and they will be pleased with you. Remember that spending quality time with your parents will make your parents happy especially when they get old, they need more of your companionship. When you were born they looked after you and when you were not even able to speak. Never call your mother and father by their names. Rather, always call them by saying, "my beloved mother" or "my beloved father."

Furthermore, we don't address our elders such as our grandparents, uncles and aunties by their names.

If your mother needs help while you are busy doing something, then you should stop doing whatever you are doing and immediately go and help her. If your father needs you whilst you are playing, then you should stop playing and go quickly to help your father. Help them to clean and tidy your house. Look after your younger brothers and sisters. These small things will make them pleased with you and they will always make Du'ā for you.

There should not be a day except that we make Du'ā for our parents, for their well-being, forgiveness, guidance and for happiness in this life and the Hereafter. Always remember that being bad to your parents is from the MAJOR SINS.

True happiness is in being obedient to Allāh, following the Sunnah of His Messenger ﷺ and being dutiful to your parents.

Our beloved Prophet ﷺ also taught us to be kind to the elderly, the young, relatives, neighbours and to our friends. We must keep in contact with our relatives, visit the sick, provide for the needy, give charity to the poor. Helping a Muslim in a time of difficulty or ease is a great charity. Smiling at a Muslim is charity.

Rights of the neighbour

Alhamdulillah the religion of Islām has taught us how to behave with all people. From the people who have a great right in Islām are our neighbours, be it Muslim or non-Muslim. The Prophet ﷺ said,

"Whoever believes in Allāh and the Last Day then let him be kind to his neighbour." (Sahīh al-Bukhārī)

In another narration, the Prophet ﷺ said three times, "By Allāh, he is not a believer."
It was asked, "Who O Messenger of Allāh?"
The Prophet ﷺ replied, "One whose neighbour does not feel safe from his evil." (Sahīh al-Bukhārī)

The way we can be good to our neighbours,

1. Saying good words to them
2. Helping them when they are in need
3. Visit them when they are sick
4. Do not cause them harm
5. Give them food especially on 'Eid
6. Teach them about our beautiful religion through your actions

Lying, Gossiping and Backbiting

The tongue is a great blessing from Allāh. This is one of the most useful parts of our body. We use it in expressing our needs and ideas in a way which pleases Allāh. Even though it is small, it is sometimes difficult to control.

The best actions one could do using their tongue is to remember Allāh, recite Qur'ān, making Du'ā and saying good words. A Muslim should always use their tongue in matters that are pleasing to Allāh. When a Muslim speaks, they speak the truth, even if by doing so they get into trouble, because Allāh will reward them greatly. We speak good words with gentleness. A Muslim does not raise their voice in front of their parents, elders and teachers.

You must also try your best to not use your tongue for things that displease Allāh such as lying, tale-carrying and backbiting etc as these are major sins.

We should not gossip as this is to talk about other people's private lives, even if it is true. We should not make fun of others. It is very important to remember that if we do not have anything good to say, then we should remain silent.

Backbiting is that you talk about another person in their absence in a way that they dislike, even if it is true. Allāh has stated in the Qur'ān that backbiting is like eating the flesh of a dead Muslim, would you like to eat the flesh of another Muslim? No you wouldn't! So stay away from backbiting.

The Prophet Muhammad ﷺ informed us that a person is punished in the grave due to tale-carrying. Backbiting and tale-carrying bring about so much harm and evil to the society. It leads to a person breaking up with his friends, people getting divorced, violence, murder and even wars between countries. This is why our religion Islām forbids these things.

Telling lies

'Abdullah ibn Mas'oud (may Allāh be pleased with him) narrated that the Prophet ﷺ said, "Truthfulness leads to righteousness and righteousness leads to Paradise. A man continues telling the truth until he is written with Allāh as a Siddeeq (truthful person). Lying leads to evil deeds and evil deeds lead to the Hell-Fire. A man continues telling lies until he is written with Allāh as a liar." (Sahīh al- Bukhārī & Muslim)

For some people lying is the easiest way to get out of trouble. In reality, lying will always place you in more trouble and create more problems. Lying is a very bad habit that leads to more lying. The more people ask you to talk, the more stories you make up. The more stories you make up, the deeper you put yourself into trouble, so always speak the truth and never lie. A common example is when someone calls or comes to your house asking for your mother or father and they tell you to tell them that they are not at home. See how easy it can be to fall into lying.

Truthfulness is one of the loftiest characters that one can have, it brings happiness in this life and the next, whereas lying is from the lowly characteristics to have, it brings misery in this life and in the Hereafter.

Remember the two angels, one on your right and one on your left writing down EVERYTHING you say and do.

Anger

Muslims should always control their anger and not say bad things when they are annoyed by others. We must be patient in difficult situations and only say things which will calm the situation. Anger often puts many people into trouble, if you were to reflect on the number of people in prison due to the effects of anger, you would seek Allāh's refuge by saying the following Du'ā when you get angry,

أَعوذُ بِاللهِ مِنَ الشَّيْطَٰنِ الرَّجِيمِ

I seek protection in Allāh from the accursed Shaytān.
(Sahīh al-Bukhārī & Sahīh al-Jaami':695)

The Prophet ﷺ told us to not be angry, if you are standing up then sit down and if you are still angry then lie down as this will stop you harming anyone with your hand or tongue. From the greatest cures of anger is that one remembers Allāh when angry. Remember that Allāh has praised those who withhold their anger. Do you want to be a strong person? Then read this hadeeth,

> "The strong man is not the one who wrestles others and beats them, rather, the strong man is the one who controls himself at the time of anger." (Sahīh Muslim)

Etiquettes of using the toilet

The Prophet Muhammad ﷺ said,

"Cleanliness is half of Eemān."

(Sahīh Muslim)

The religion of Islām encourages us to be clean at all times.

When going to the toilet,

1. Do not carry anything with you that has Allāh's Name on it.
2. Take enough water with you to wash yourself.
3. Step into the toilet with your left foot and say,

اللَّهُمَّ إِنِّي أَعُوذُ بِكَ مِنَ الْخُبُثِ وَالْخَبَائِثِ

"O Allāh, I take refuge with You from male and female devils."
(Sahīh al-Bukhārī)

4. You should not talk when in the toilet, or respond to others' greetings.
5. It is better to urinate whilst sitting so that the urine does not splash on your body or clothing.
6. It is best not to urinate while standing.
7. After relieving yourself, clean yourself properly with water.
8. If you are using tissue paper, make sure to wipe yourself at least three times, with a fresh tissue each time.

9. Wash your hands after using the toilet.
10. Come out of the toilet with your right foot first, saying,

غُفْـرَانَكَ

"I ask you (O Allāh) for forgiveness."
(Tirmidhi:7)

It is from good manners after using the toilet to make sure it is left clean and tidy.

How would you feel if you found the toilet dirty and messy?

You would not like it, so likewise do not leave it dirty and messy for others.

Etiquette of eating and drinking

1. You should wash your hands properly before eating.
2. Before you eat or drink you should say,

بِسْمِ اللهِ

"I begin in the Name of Allāh" (Abū Dāwūd:3767)

3. You should eat and drink with your right hand.
4. Drink water in three sips.
5. It is better to sit down when eating or drinking.
6. Eat small morsels of food and chew well before swallowing.
7. You should eat that which is closest to you.
8. If the food or drink is hot then you should not blow on it to cool it, wait until it cools down.
9. The Prophet Muhammad ﷺ forbade us from eating or drinking with the left hand as Shaytān eats and drinks with his left hand.
10. You should only take enough food and drink for yourself which will satisfy your hunger and thirst.

The Prophet Muhammad ﷺ never spoke badly about food or criticise it because food is a blessing from Allāh. It may be that the food you criticise today will not be available tomorrow when you have no other food. Criticising food means that you do not appreciate Allāh's blessings. We should always show gratefulness to Allāh for His countless blessings.

When you finish eating a meal say,

الْحَمْدُ لِلَّهِ الَّذِي أَطْعَمَنِي هَـذَا وَرَزَقَنِيهِ مِنْ غَيْرِ حَوْلٍ مِنِّي وَلَا قُوَّة

"All praise is for Allāh who fed me this and granted it as provision to me, without any effort from me nor power."

The Prophet Muhammad ﷺ said, whoever says the above Du'ā after finishing a meal, "his past sins shall be forgiven." (Tirmidhi:3458)

How kind is Allah! He provides for us and then forgives us for acknowledging and giving thanks for the blessing of provision.

In this Du'ā the Prophet ﷺ taught us to offer thanks to Allāh for the food that He provided us and the ease with which it is digested, benefitting the body with its nutrients and the body's rejection of its harmful waste.

How can we worship other than Allāh? The One Who provides for all of His creation and this does not decrease His Dominion whatsoever.

Etiquettes of sleeping

Islām teaches us the best of manners to be a better Muslim in the society we live in. As Muslims we must behave in a manner which pleases our Lord. Our day should start and finish with obedience to Allāh. Our dealing with our parents, teachers, neighbours, friends, families, Muslims and non-Muslims should be according to the teachings of Islām which is to be kind, merciful and just with everyone.

We will now briefly discuss those things which will make you a better Muslim, thereby making you a good person and a good member of the community. May Allāh give you success. (Āmeen)

Our beloved Prophet Muhammad ﷺ told us the mannerism of going to bed and how to sleep.

1. Before lying on the bed, one should shake his mattress with his garment three times, saying each time,

   بِسْمِ اللهِ

   "In the Name of Allāh."

2. Make sure your bed is clean before you sleep.
3. Make sure you sleep early after having prayed 'Ishaa' so that you can be fresh and ready for the next day starting with the Fajr prayer.

4. It is recommended to make Wudhu before you sleep. If you do so, an angel will be sent to protect you until the morning.
5. You should sleep on your right side and place your right hand under your right cheek.
6. We should not sleep on our stomach.
7. Before sleeping the Prophet ﷺ would hold his palms together, blow (a form of spitting comprising mainly of air with little spittle) in them, recite the last three chapters of al-Qur'ān (Al-Ikhlās, Al-Falaq, An-Nās) and then wipe over his entire body as much as possible with his hands, beginning with his head and face and then all parts of the body, he would do this three times.
8. He would also recite Āyatul-Kursi and the last two Āyahs of Sūrah al-Baqarah.
9. He would also say the following Du'ā when sleeping,

بِاسْمِكَ اللَّهُمَّ أَمُوتُ وَأَحْيَا

"In your Name O Allāh, I live and die." (Sahīh al-Bukhārī)

10. When waking up, say the following Du'ā,

الحَمْدُ لِلَّهِ الَّذِي أَحْيَانَا بَعْدَ مَا أَمَاتَنَا وَإِلَيهِ النُّشُور

"All praise is for Allāh who gave us life after having taken it from us and unto Him is the resurrection." (Sahīh al-Bukhārī)

Islamic calendar

The Islamic calendar is also called the Hijri calendar which also has 12 months, but unlike the Gregorion calendar, it has approximately 355 days. This is because the Hijri calendar follows the movements of the earth's moon. The Hijri calendar began in the year in which our beloved Prophet Muhammad ﷺ emigrated from Makkah to Madeenah.

Each month of the Islamic calendar officially begins when the lunar crescent is seen with the naked eye. This is not always an exact time, especially if the skies are cloudy. An Islamic month can be 29 or 30 days.

The 12 months of the Islamic calendar, in order are listed below.

1. Al-Muharram	2. Safar	3. Rabi' al-Awwal
4. Rabi' al-Ākhir	5. Jumada al-Awwal	6. Jumada al-Ākhir
7. Rajab	8. Sha'bān	9. Ramadān
10.Shawwāl	11. Dhul-Qa'dah	12. Dhul-Hijjah

There are two 'Eids in the Islamic calendar:

- 'Eid ul-Fitr (1st of Shawwāl after the completion of Ramadān)

- ‘Eid ul-Adha (10th of Dhul-Hijjah)

Write the months in the correct order

Jumada al- Ākhir	1.
Dhul-Hijjah	2.
Safar	3.
Shawwal	4.
Rabi' ul-Awwal	5.
Sha'bān	6.
Jumada al-Awwal	7.
Al-Muharram	8.
Rajab	9.
Rabi' al- Ākhir	10.
Ramadān	11.
Dhul-Qa'dah	12.

What is today’s Islamic date?

DD/MM/YY: ___ /___ /___

Write down your date of birth according to Islamic calendar:

DD/MM/YY: ___ /___ /___

Daily remembrances for morning and evening

Read Āyatul-Kursi (once) (Sahīh at-Targheeb wat-Tarheeb no:661)

Sūrah al-Ikhlās, Sūrah al-Falaq and Sūrah an-Nās (3 times) (Tirmidhi:3575)

O Ever-Living One! O Self-Subsisting Sustainer of everything! By Your mercy I beseech: rectify for me all of my affairs, and do not entrust me to my own self for the blink of an eye. (Sahīh at-Targheeb wat-Tarheeb no:661)

يَا حَيُّ يَا قَيُّومُ بِرَحْمَتِكَ أَسْتَغِيثُ، أَصْلِحْ لِي شَأْنِي كُلَّهُ، وَلَا تَكِلْنِي إِلَى نَفْسِي طَرْفَةَ عَيْنٍ

In the Name of Allāh, He Whose Name is such that when it is mentioned nothing in the earth or the heavens can cause harm and He is the All-Hearing, the All-Knowing. (3 times) (Abū Dāwūd:5088)

بِسْمِ اللهِ الَّذِي لَا يَضُرُّ مَعَ اسْمِهِ شَيْءٌ فِي الْأَرْضِ وَلَا فِي السَّمَاءِ وَهُوَ السَّمِيعُ الْعَلِيم

I am pleased and satisfied with Allāh as my Lord and Islām as my religion and Muhammad ﷺ as my Prophet. (once in the morning only) (as-Saheehah:2686)

رَضِيتُ بِاللهِ رَبًّا وَبِالْإِسْلَامِ دِينًا وَبِمُحَمَّدٍ نَبِيًّا

I seek refuge in the perfect and complete Words of Allāh from the evil of whatever He has created. (3 times in the evening only) (Tirmidhi:3604)

أَعُوذُ بِكَلِمَاتِ اللهِ التَّامَّاتِ مِنْ شَرِّ مَا خَلَق

Other Supplications

1. When leaving home

With the Name of Allāh, I place my trust in Allāh, there is no change and no ability except with (Help of) Allāh. (Tirmidhi:3462)

بِسْمِ اللهِ، تَوَكَّلْتُ عَلَى اللهِ وَلَا حَوْلَ وَلَا قُوَّةَ إِلَّا بِاللهِ

2. When visiting the sick

Don't worry, it (the sickness) is a purification (for your sins), if Allāh wills. (Sahīh al-Bukhārī)

لَا بَأْسَ طَهُورٌ إِنْ شَاءَ اللهُ

3. When it rains

O Allāh, may it be a beneficial rain. (Abū Dāwūd:5099)

اللَّهُمَّ صَيِّباً نَافِعاً

4. Upon sneezing (When one of you sneezes he should say)

"All praise is for Allāh."

الْحَمْدُ لِلَّهِ

(and the one who hears this, says to him)

"May Allāh have mercy upon you."

يَرْحَمُكَ اللهُ

(and the one who sneezed replies to him)

"May Allāh guide you and rectify your affairs." (Sahīh al-Bukhārī)

يَهْدِيكُمُ اللهُ وَيُصْلِحُ بَالَكُم

5. To one who does good to you

"May Allāh reward you with goodness." (Tirmidhi:2035)

جَزَاكَ اللهُ خَيْراً

6 - Excellence of remembrance and glorification of Allāh

Abū Hurayrah reported that the Messenger of Allāh ﷺ said: "(There are) two words, (which are) light on the tongue, heavy on the scale and beloved to The Most Merciful",

سُبْحَانَ اللهِ وَبِحَمْدِهِ وَسُبْحَانَ اللهِ العَظِيمِ

"I declare Allāh free of all imperfections and all praise is for Him. I declare Allāh free of all imperfections, The Magnificient One." (Sahīh al-Bukhārī)

Abū Hurayrah reported that the Messenger of Allāh said: "Saying ...

سُبْحَانَ اللهِ، وَالحَمْدُ للهِ، وَلَآ إِلَهَ إِلَّا اللهُ وَاللهُ أَكْبَرُ

'I declare Allāh free of all imperfections, and all praise is for Allāh. None has the right to be worshipped except Allāh, and Allāh is the Greatest.'

...is more beloved to me than everything the sun has risen over." (Sahīh Muslim)

The Prophet Muhammad ﷺ said, say,

لَا حَوْلَ وَلَا قُوَّةَ إِلَّا بِاللهِ

"There is no change and no ability except with (Help of) Allāh."

For it is a treasure from the treasures of Paradise.
(Sahīh al-Bukhārī & Sahīh Muslim)

Sūrahs from Qur'ān

سُورَةُ الفَاتِحَة

In the Name of Allāh, the Most-Merciful, the Bestower of Mercy.	بِسۡمِ ٱللَّهِ ٱلرَّحۡمَٰنِ ٱلرَّحِيمِ ١
All praise is for Allāh, the Lord of all creation.	ٱلۡحَمۡدُ لِلَّهِ رَبِّ ٱلۡعَٰلَمِينَ ٢
The Most Merciful, the Bestower of Mercy.	ٱلرَّحۡمَٰنِ ٱلرَّحِيمِ ٣
The Only Owner (and the Only Ruling Judge) of the Day of Recompense (i.e. the Day of Resurrection).	مَٰلِكِ يَوۡمِ ٱلدِّينِ ٤
You (alone) we worship, and You (alone) we ask for help (for each and everything).	إِيَّاكَ نَعۡبُدُ وَإِيَّاكَ نَسۡتَعِينُ ٥
Guide us to the Straight Way.	ٱهۡدِنَا ٱلصِّرَٰطَ ٱلۡمُسۡتَقِيمَ ٦
The Way of those on whom You have bestowed Your Grace, not (the way) of those who earned Your Anger, nor of those who went astray.	صِرَٰطَ ٱلَّذِينَ أَنۡعَمۡتَ عَلَيۡهِمۡ غَيۡرِ ٱلۡمَغۡضُوبِ عَلَيۡهِمۡ وَلَا ٱلضَّآلِّينَ ٧

آيَةُ الكُرْسِيِّ

ٱللَّهُ لَآ إِلَٰهَ إِلَّا هُوَ ٱلۡحَيُّ ٱلۡقَيُّومُۚ لَا تَأۡخُذُهُۥ سِنَةٞ وَلَا نَوۡمٞۚ لَّهُۥ مَا فِي ٱلسَّمَٰوَٰتِ وَمَا فِي ٱلۡأَرۡضِۗ

Allāh! None has the right to be worshipped except Him; the Ever-Living, the Self-Substing Sustainer of all that exists. Neither drowsiness nor sleep overtakes Him. To Him belongs whatever is in the heavens and whatever is in the earth.

مَن ذَا ٱلَّذِي يَشۡفَعُ عِندَهُۥٓ إِلَّا بِإِذۡنِهِۦۚ يَعۡلَمُ مَا بَيۡنَ أَيۡدِيهِمۡ وَمَا خَلۡفَهُمۡۖ

None can intercede with Him except with His Permission. He knows what happens to them (His creatures) in this world, and what will happen to them in the Hereafter.

وَلَا يُحِيطُونَ بِشَيۡءٖ مِّنۡ عِلۡمِهِۦٓ إِلَّا بِمَا شَآءَۚ وَسِعَ كُرۡسِيُّهُ ٱلسَّمَٰوَٰتِ وَٱلۡأَرۡضَۖ

And they cannot encompass anything of His Knowledge except that which He wills. His Footstool extends over the heavens and the earth,

وَلَا يَـُٔودُهُۥ حِفۡظُهُمَاۚ وَهُوَ ٱلۡعَلِيُّ ٱلۡعَظِيمُ ٢٥٥

And He feels no fatigue in guarding and preserving them. And He is the Most High, the Magnificient. (Al-Baqarah:255)

سُورَةُ الْقَارِعَةِ

In the Name of Allāh, the Most-Merciful, the Bestower of Mercy.	بِسْمِ اللَّهِ الرَّحْمَٰنِ الرَّحِيمِ
Al-Qaari'ah (the striking Hour i.e. the Day of Resurrection)	الْقَارِعَةُ ﴿١﴾
What is the striking (Hour)?	مَا الْقَارِعَةُ ﴿٢﴾
And what will make you know what the striking (Hour) is?	وَمَا أَدْرَاكَ مَا الْقَارِعَةُ ﴿٣﴾
It is a Day when mankind will be like moths scattered about.	يَوْمَ يَكُونُ النَّاسُ كَالْفَرَاشِ الْمَبْثُوثِ ﴿٤﴾
And the mountains will be like carded wool.	وَتَكُونُ الْجِبَالُ كَالْعِهْنِ الْمَنفُوشِ ﴿٥﴾
Then as for him whose balance (of good deeds) will be heavy.	فَأَمَّا مَن ثَقُلَتْ مَوَازِينُهُ ﴿٦﴾
He will live a pleasant life (in Paradise).	فَهُوَ فِي عِيشَةٍ رَّاضِيَةٍ ﴿٧﴾
But as for him whose balance (of good deeds) will be light.	وَأَمَّا مَنْ خَفَّتْ مَوَازِينُهُ ﴿٨﴾
He will have his home in Hawiyah (pit, i.e. Hell).	فَأُمُّهُ هَاوِيَةٌ ﴿٩﴾

And what will make you know what it is?	وَمَآ أَدۡرَىٰكَ مَا هِيَهۡ ١٠
(It is) a fierce blazing Fire!	نَارٌ حَامِيَةُۢ ١١

سُورَةُ التَّكَاثُر

In the Name of Allāh, the Most-Merciful, the Bestower of Mercy.	بِسۡمِ ٱللَّهِ ٱلرَّحۡمَٰنِ ٱلرَّحِيمِ
The mutual rivalry (for piling up of worldly things) diverts you.	أَلۡهَىٰكُمُ ٱلتَّكَاثُرُ ١
Until you visit the graves. (i.e. when you die)	حَتَّىٰ زُرۡتُمُ ٱلۡمَقَابِرَ ٢
Rather! You shall come to know!	كَلَّا سَوۡفَ تَعۡلَمُونَ ٣
Again, Rather! You shall come to know!	ثُمَّ كَلَّا سَوۡفَ تَعۡلَمُونَ ٤
Rather! If you knew with a sure knowledge (the end result of piling up, you would not have occupied yourselves in worldly things).	كَلَّا لَوۡ تَعۡلَمُونَ عِلۡمَ ٱلۡيَقِينِ ٥
Verily, You shall see the blazing Fire (Hell)!	لَتَرَوُنَّ ٱلۡجَحِيمَ ٦

And again, you shall see it with certainty of sight!	ثُمَّ لَتَرَوُنَّهَا عَيْنَ ٱلْيَقِينِ ٧
Then, on that Day, you shall be asked about the delights (you indulged in, in this world)!	ثُمَّ لَتُسْـَٔلُنَّ يَوْمَئِذٍ عَنِ ٱلنَّعِيمِ ٨

سُورَةُ العَصر

In the Name of Allāh, the Most-Merciful, the Bestower of Mercy.	بِسْمِ ٱللَّهِ ٱلرَّحْمَٰنِ ٱلرَّحِيمِ
By time.	وَٱلْعَصْرِ ١
Mankind is in loss.	إِنَّ ٱلْإِنسَٰنَ لَفِى خُسْرٍ ٢
Except for those who truly and correctly believe (and worship Allāh alone) and do righteous deeds (performing that which is obligatory upon them and avoiding that which they are forbidden from) and enjoin one another with the truth and enjoin one another with patient perseverance upon obedience to Allāh and in facing harms and trial.	إِلَّا ٱلَّذِينَ ءَامَنُوا۟ وَعَمِلُوا۟ ٱلصَّٰلِحَٰتِ وَتَوَاصَوْا۟ بِٱلْحَقِّ وَتَوَاصَوْا۟ بِٱلصَّبْرِ ٣

سُورَةُ الهُمَزَة

In the Name of Allāh, the Most-Merciful, the Bestower of Mercy.	بِسۡمِ اللهِ الرَّحۡمٰنِ الرَّحِيۡمِ
Woe to every slanderer and backbiter.	وَيۡلٞ لِّكُلِّ هُمَزَةٖ لُّمَزَةٍ ١
Who has gathered wealth and continuously counts it.	ٱلَّذِي جَمَعَ مَالٗا وَعَدَّدَهُۥ ٢
He thinks that his wealth will make him last forever!	يَحۡسَبُ أَنَّ مَالَهُۥٓ أَخۡلَدَهُۥ ٣
Rather! Verily, he will be thrown into the crushing Fire.	كَلَّاۖ لَيُنۢبَذَنَّ فِي ٱلۡحُطَمَةِ ٤
And what will make you know what the crushing Fire is?	وَمَآ أَدۡرَىٰكَ مَا ٱلۡحُطَمَةُ ٥
The Fire of Allāh, kindled.	نَارُ ٱللَّهِ ٱلۡمُوقَدَةُ ٦
Which leaps up over the hearts.	ٱلَّتِي تَطَّلِعُ عَلَى ٱلۡأَفۡـِٔدَةِ ٧
Verily, it shall be closed upon them.	إِنَّهَا عَلَيۡهِم مُّؤۡصَدَةٞ ٨
In pillars stretched forth (i.e. they will be punished in the Fire with pillars).	فِي عَمَدٖ مُّمَدَّدَةِۭ ٩

سُورَةُ ٱلْفِيلِ

In the Name of Allāh, the Most-Merciful, the Bestower of Mercy.	بِسۡمِ ٱللَّهِ ٱلرَّحۡمَٰنِ ٱلرَّحِيمِ
Have you (O Muhammad ﷺ) not seen how your Lord dealt with the Owners of the Elephant? [The elephant army which came from Yemen under the command of Abrahah (Al-Ashram) intending to destroy the K'abah at Makkah].	أَلَمۡ تَرَ كَيۡفَ فَعَلَ رَبُّكَ بِأَصۡحَٰبِ ٱلۡفِيلِ ١
Did He not make their plot go astray?	أَلَمۡ يَجۡعَلۡ كَيۡدَهُمۡ فِي تَضۡلِيلٖ ٢
And He sent against them birds, in flocks.	وَأَرۡسَلَ عَلَيۡهِمۡ طَيۡرًا أَبَابِيلَ ٣
Striking them with stones of Sijjeel (baked clay).	تَرۡمِيهِم بِحِجَارَةٖ مِّن سِجِّيلٖ ٤
And He made them like an empty field of stalks (of which the corn has been eaten up by cattle).	فَجَعَلَهُمۡ كَعَصۡفٖ مَّأۡكُولِۭ ٥

سُورَةُ قُرَيْش

In the Name of Allāh, the Most-Merciful, the Bestower of Mercy.	بِسۡمِ ٱللَّهِ ٱلرَّحۡمَٰنِ ٱلرَّحِيمِ
For the protection of the Quraysh.	لِإِيلَٰفِ قُرَيۡشٍ ﴿١﴾
We cause the (Quraysh) caravans to set forth safe in winter (to the south), and in summer (to the north without any fear).	إِۦلَٰفِهِمۡ رِحۡلَةَ ٱلشِّتَآءِ وَٱلصَّيۡفِ ﴿٢﴾
So let them worship (Allāh) the Lord of this House (the K'abah in Makkah).	فَلۡيَعۡبُدُواْ رَبَّ هَٰذَا ٱلۡبَيۡتِ ﴿٣﴾
Who has fed them against hunger, and has made them safe from fear.	ٱلَّذِيٓ أَطۡعَمَهُم مِّن جُوعٖ وَءَامَنَهُم مِّنۡ خَوۡفِۭ ﴿٤﴾

سُورَةُ الْمَاعُون

In the Name of Allāh, the Most-Merciful, the Bestower of Mercy.	بِسۡمِ ٱللَّهِ ٱلرَّحۡمَٰنِ ٱلرَّحِيمِ
Have you seen him who denies the Recompense? (i.e. the Day of Judgement)	أَرَءَيۡتَ ٱلَّذِي يُكَذِّبُ بِٱلدِّينِ ﴿١﴾

That is he who drives away the orphan (harshly).	فَذَٰلِكَ الَّذِي يَدُعُّ الْيَتِيمَ ﴿٢﴾
And does not encourage the feeding of the poor.	وَلَا يَحُضُّ عَلَىٰ طَعَامِ الْمِسْكِينِ ﴿٣﴾
So woe unto those who perform the Salaat (prayers).	فَوَيْلٌ لِّلْمُصَلِّينَ ﴿٤﴾
Those who delay their prayer (from their stated fixed times and are careless).	الَّذِينَ هُمْ عَن صَلَاتِهِمْ سَاهُونَ ﴿٥﴾
Those who do good deeds only to be seen of people.	الَّذِينَ هُمْ يُرَاءُونَ ﴿٦﴾
And withold Al-Maa'oun (small kindnesses like salt, sugar, water) from the people.	وَيَمْنَعُونَ الْمَاعُونَ ﴿٧﴾

سُورَةُ الْكَوْثَر

In the Name of Allāh, the Most-Merciful, the Bestower of Mercy.	بِسْمِ اللَّهِ الرَّحْمَٰنِ الرَّحِيمِ
Verily, We have granted you (O Muhammad ﷺ) Al-Kauthar (a river in Paradise).	إِنَّا أَعْطَيْنَاكَ الْكَوْثَرَ ﴿١﴾
Therefore turn in prayer to your Lord and sacrifice (to Him only).	فَصَلِّ لِرَبِّكَ وَانْحَرْ ﴿٢﴾

For he who hates you (O Muhammad ﷺ), he will be cut off from every posterity (good thing in this world and in the Hereafter)	إِنَّ شَانِئَكَ هُوَ ٱلْأَبْتَرُ ٣

سُورَةُ الكافِرُون

In the Name of Allāh, the Most-Merciful, the Bestower of Mercy.	بِسْمِ ٱللَّهِ ٱلرَّحْمَٰنِ ٱلرَّحِيمِ
Say (O Muhammad ﷺ): "O Al-Kaafiroon (disbelievers in Allāh, in His Oneness, in His Angels, in His Books, in His Messengers, in the Day of Resurrection, and in Al-Qadar)!	قُلْ يَٰٓأَيُّهَا ٱلْكَٰفِرُونَ ١
I worship not that which you worship.	لَآ أَعْبُدُ مَا تَعْبُدُونَ ٢
Nor do you worship that which I worship.	وَلَآ أَنتُمْ عَٰبِدُونَ مَآ أَعْبُدُ ٣
And I shall not worship that which you are worshipping.	وَلَآ أَنَا۠ عَابِدٌ مَّا عَبَدتُّمْ ٤
Nor will you worship that which I worship.	وَلَآ أَنتُمْ عَٰبِدُونَ مَآ أَعْبُدُ ٥

To you be your religion, and to me my religion (Islamic Monotheism).	لَكُمۡ دِينُكُمۡ وَلِيَ دِينِ ٦

سُورَةُ النَّصر

In the Name of Allāh, the Most-Merciful, the Bestower of Mercy.	بِسۡمِ ٱللَّهِ ٱلرَّحۡمَٰنِ ٱلرَّحِيمِ
When there comes the Help of Allāh (to you, O Muhammad ﷺ and the Conquest (of Makkah).	إِذَا جَآءَ نَصۡرُ ٱللَّهِ وَٱلۡفَتۡحُ ١
And you see that the people enter Allāh's religion (Islām) in crowds.	وَرَأَيۡتَ ٱلنَّاسَ يَدۡخُلُونَ فِي دِينِ ٱللَّهِ أَفۡوَاجٗا ٢
So glorify the praises of your Lord, and ask His Forgiveness. Verily, He is the One Who accepts the repentance and Who forgives.	فَسَبِّحۡ بِحَمۡدِ رَبِّكَ وَٱسۡتَغۡفِرۡهُۚ إِنَّهُۥ كَانَ تَوَّابَۢا ٣

سُورَةُ المَسَد

In the Name of Allāh, the Most-Merciful, the Bestower of Mercy.	بِسۡمِ ٱللَّهِ ٱلرَّحۡمَٰنِ ٱلرَّحِيمِ
Perish the two hands of abū Lahab, and	تَبَّتۡ يَدَآ أَبِي لَهَبٖ وَتَبَّ ١

perish he!	
His wealth and his children will not benefit him!	مَآ أَغْنَىٰ عَنْهُ مَالُهُۥ وَمَا كَسَبَ ﴿٢﴾
He will be burnt in a Fire of blazing flames!	سَيَصْلَىٰ نَارًا ذَاتَ لَهَبٍ ﴿٣﴾
And his wife too, who carries wood (thorns of Sadan which she used to put on the way of the Prophet ﷺ, or use to slander him).	وَامْرَأَتُهُۥ حَمَّالَةَ الْحَطَبِ ﴿٤﴾
In her neck is a twisted rope of Masad (palm fibre).	فِى جِيدِهَا حَبْلٌ مِّن مَّسَدٍۭ ﴿٥﴾

سُورَةُ الْإِخْلَاص

In the Name of Allāh, the Most-Merciful, the Bestower of Mercy.	بِسْمِ اللَّهِ الرَّحْمَٰنِ الرَّحِيمِ
Say (O Muhammad ﷺ): "He is Allāh, (the) One and Unique.	قُلْ هُوَ اللَّهُ أَحَدٌ ﴿١﴾
Allāh-us-Samad (Allāh the Self-Sufficient Master, Whom all creatures need, (He neither eats nor drinks)).	اللَّهُ الصَّمَدُ ﴿٢﴾
He begets not, nor was He begotten.	لَمْ يَلِدْ وَلَمْ يُولَدْ ﴿٣﴾

And there is none co-equal or comparable unto Him."	وَلَمْ يَكُن لَّهُۥ كُفُوًا أَحَدٌۢ ﴿٤﴾

سُورَةُ الفَلَق

In the Name of Allāh, the Most-Merciful, the Bestower of Mercy.	بِسْمِ ٱللَّهِ ٱلرَّحْمَٰنِ ٱلرَّحِيمِ
Say: "I seek refuge with (Allāh) the Lord of the daybreak.	قُلْ أَعُوذُ بِرَبِّ ٱلْفَلَقِ ﴿١﴾
"From the evil of what He has created.	مِن شَرِّ مَا خَلَقَ ﴿٢﴾
And from the evil of the darkening (night) as it comes with its darkness.	وَمِن شَرِّ غَاسِقٍ إِذَا وَقَبَ ﴿٣﴾
And from the evil of those who practice witchcraft when they blow in the knots.	وَمِن شَرِّ ٱلنَّفَّٰثَٰتِ فِى ٱلْعُقَدِ ﴿٤﴾
And from the evil of the envier when he envies."	وَمِن شَرِّ حَاسِدٍ إِذَا حَسَدَ ﴿٥﴾

سُورَةُ النَّاس

In the Name of Allāh, the Most-Merciful, the Bestower of Mercy.	بِسْمِ اللهِ الرَّحْمَٰنِ الرَّحِيمِ
Say: "I seek refuge with (Allāh) the Lord of mankind.	قُلْ أَعُوذُ بِرَبِّ النَّاسِ ١
The King of mankind.	مَلِكِ النَّاسِ ٢
The Ilaah (God) of mankind.	إِلَٰهِ النَّاسِ ٣
From the evil of the whisperer who withdraws (from his whispering in one's heart after one remembers Allāh).	مِن شَرِّ الْوَسْوَاسِ الْخَنَّاسِ ٤
Who whispers in the breasts of mankind.	الَّذِي يُوَسْوِسُ فِي صُدُورِ النَّاسِ ٥
Of jinn and men."	مِنَ الْجِنَّةِ وَالنَّاسِ ٦

General Questions

1. Who is our Lord?
2. Who created everything?
3. What is your religion?
4. Who is your Prophet?
5. What is the name of our Holy Book?
6. Which angel is responsible for bringing the revelation to the Prophets?
7. How many months are there in the Islamic calender?
8. Islām is built upon how many pillars?
9. How many pillars of Eemān are there?
10. Who gives life and death?
11. Where was Prophet Muhammad ﷺ born?
12. When do Muslims fast?
13. How many 'Eids do we have in a year?
14. Who built the K'abah?
15. Who was the first man Allāh created?
16. Which Prophet was ordered by Allāh to build a ship?
17. Which Prophet was swallowed by a whale?
18. How many angels will question you in the grave?
19. Who is 'Isa عليه السلام?
20. Which Prophet was sent to the people of Isrā'īl?

21. Which Prophet knew the languages of the birds and animals?
22. Which city did Prophet Muhammad ﷺ migrate to?
23. Which year did Muhammad ﷺ migrate from Makkah?
24. Who accompanied him on this journey?
25. Over How many years was the Qur'ān revealed to the Prophet Muhammad ﷺ?
26. How many Juz' are there in the Qur'ān?
27. How many Sūrahs are there in the Qur'ān?
28. Which is the longest Sūrah in the Qur'ān?
29. Which is the shortest Sūrah in the Qur'ān?
30. What is the greatest Āyah in the Qur'ān?
31. What is the name of the first Sūrah revealed to Prophet Muhammad ﷺ?
32. How many Sūrahs have you memorised from the Qur'ān?
33. What is our belief regarding the Qur'ān?
34. Does Allāh have any children?
35. Is Prophet Muhammad ﷺ still alive in this world?
36. Is Allāh everywhere?
37. Where is Allāh?
38. Why did Allāh create mankind and jinn?
39. What did Allāh create the angels from?
40. What did Allāh create Ādam from?

41. Who knows when the Day of Judgement will be?
42. In how many days did Allāh create the heavens and the earths?
43. What is the greatest sin?
44. Inventing new things in the religion is called?
45. How many types of Sunnah are there?
46. Who is the best Prophet?
47. Who revealed the Qur'ān?
48. At what age did Muhammad ﷺ become a Prophet of Allāh?
49. How many times a day do we pray?
50. Where do Muslims go for Hajj?
51. Can you name 15 Prophets?
52. Who is a Sahaabi?
53. Can you name 15 Sahaabah?
54. Did Prophet Muhammad ﷺ know the unseen completely?
55. Can we ask others for help besides Allāh?
56. What do we say before we eat or drink?
57. Which hand do we eat and drink with?
58. What name is given to the person who calls the Adhān?
59. What name is given to the person who leads the prayer?
60. What is the place where Muslims pray called?

61. Did ‘Isa ﷺ die on the cross?
62. What is the command which Allāh uses to create everything from nothing?
63. Name 10 things from your surroundings that you can see which Allāh created?
64. Can you name 5 things which you cannot see that Allāh created?
65. Who was the first Caliph in Islām after the death of Prophet Muhammad ﷺ?
66. Who was the second Caliph?
67. Who was the third Caliph?
68. Who was the fourth Caliph?
69. Where do we take our knowledge of Islām from?
70. Who is the last of all Prophets and Messengers?
71. What is the name of the prayer which is prayed after ‘Ishaa’ prayer in Ramadān?
72. How many children did Prophet Muhammad ﷺ have?
73. Name the wives of Prophet Muhammad ﷺ?
74. What should one say upon hearing the name of our Prophet ﷺ?
75. What did Allāh order us with regarding our parents?
76. At what age did Prophet Muhammad ﷺ die?
77. Where is he (Muhammad ﷺ) buried?

78. Can you name 2 holy Masajid?
79. What should one say after drinking and eating?
80. What should one say upon entering the toilet?
81. What is the Du'ā after completing the Wudhu?
82. How should one enter and leave the Masjid?
83. What did Prophet Muhammad ﷺ say about how to pray?
84. Who were the Ashara Mubasharah promised Paradise?
85. How old was Prophet Muhammad ﷺ when his mother died?
86. When did the Prophet's ﷺ wife Khadījah رضي الله عنها die?
87. Who was the father of 'Ā'ishah رضي الله عنها?
88. What did Allāh order Ibrāhīm عليه السلام to sacrifice?
89. What is the Sunnah?
90. Calling upon other than Allāh is?
91. From what age should the child learn how to pray?
92. What breaks the Wudhu?
93. Name a few books which Allāh revealed to His Messengers?
94. What is ZamZam?
95. Where is Safa and Marwa?
96. When do we celebrate 'Eid ul-Fitr and 'Eid al-Adha?
97. What is the most important thing one should learn about?

98. Who is most deserving of our kindness?
99. What Du'ā do we say before going to bed?
100. What did Allāh create Shaytān from?

Let's learn some Arabic

Days of the week		أَيَّامُ الأُسْبُوعِ	
Sunday	يَوْمُ الأَحَدِ	Monday	يَوْمُ الإِثْنَيْنِ
Tuesday	يَوْمُ الثُّلَاثَاءِ	Wednesday	يَوْمُ الأَرْبِعَاءِ
Thursday	يَوْمُ الخَمِيسِ	Friday	يَوْمُ الجُمُعَةِ
Saturday	يَوْمُ السَّبْتِ		
*Month	شَهْرٌ	*Year	عَامٌ

Times of the day		مُفْرَدَاتُ الزَّمَنِ	
Dawn	فَجْرٌ	Sunrise	شُرُوقٌ
Morning	صَبَاحٌ	Noon	ظُهْرٌ
Afternoon	عَصْرٌ	Evening	مَسَاءٌ

Sunset	مَغْرِبٌ	Night-time	لَيْلٌ

Family Members			أَفْرَادُ الْأُسْرَةِ
Mother	أُمٌّ	Father	أَبٌ
Sister	أُخْتٌ	Brother	أَخٌ
Daughter	بِنْتٌ	Son	اِبْنٌ
Aunt (paternal)	عَمَّةٌ	Uncle (paternal)	عَمٌّ
Aunt (maternal)	خَالَةٌ	Uncle (Maternal)	خَالٌ
Grandmother	جَدَّةٌ	Grandfather	جَدٌّ

Fruits			ثِمَارٌ
Apple	تُفَّاحٌ	Banana	مَوْزٌ
Cherry	كَرَزٌ	Date	تَمْرٌ

Grape	عِنَبٌ	Fig	تِين
Orange	بُرْتُقَالٌ	Pineapple	أَنَانَاسٌ
Pomegranate	رُمَّانٌ	Strawberry	فَرَاوِلَةٌ

Numbers		أَعدَاد	
1	وَاحِد	2	اِثْنَانِ
3	ثَلَاثَةٌ	4	أَرْبَعَةٌ
5	خَمْسَةٌ	6	سِتَّةٌ
7	سَبْعَةٌ	8	ثَمَانِيَةٌ
9	تِسْعَةٌ	10	عَشَرَةٌ

Animals		مُفْرَدَاتُ الحَيَوَانَات	
Bear	دُبٌّ	Chicken	دَجَاجَةٌ

Cow	بَقَرَةٌ	Duck	بَطَّةٌ
Donkey	حِمَارٌ	Elephant	فِيلٌ
Giraffe	زَرَافَةٌ	Horse	حِصَانٌ
Lion	أَسَدٌ	Monkey	قِرْدٌ
Pig	خِنْزِيرٌ	Rooster	دِيك
Sheep	خَرُوفٌ	Wolf	الذِّئْبُ

Colours		أَلْوَانٌ	
Red	أَحْمَرُ	Brown	بُنِّيٌّ
Orange	البُرْتُقَالِيُّ	Yellow	أَصْفَرُ
Green	أَخْضَرُ	Blue	أَزْرَقُ
Purple	أُرْجُوَانِيٌّ	Pink	وَرْدِيٌّ
Black	أَسْوَدُ	White	أَبْيَضُ

Body parts		مُفْرَدَاتُ جِسْمِ الإِنْسَانُ	
Ear	أُذُنٌ	Chest	صَدْرٌ
Face	وَجْهٌ	Eye	عَيْنٌ
Foot	قَدَمٌ	Hair	شَعْرٌ
Hand	يَدٌ	Head	رَأْسٌ
Heart	قَلْبٌ	Knee	رُكْبَةٌ
Leg	رِجْلٌ	Lip	شَفَةٌ
Mouth	فَمٌ	Nose	أَنْفٌ
Throat	حَلْقٌ	Thumb	إِبْهَامٌ
Tongue	لِسَانٌ	Tooth	سِنٌّ

Arabic Vocabulary		المُفْرَدَاتُ العَرَبِيَّةُ	
Airplane	طَائِرَةٌ	Airport	مَطَارٌ

Bicycle	دَرَّاجَةٌ	Book	كِتَابٌ
Bus	حَافِلَةٌ	Bread	خُبْزٌ
Car	سَيَّارَةٌ	Chair	كُرْسِيٌّ
Clock	سَاعَةٌ	Door	بَابٌ
Football	كُرَةُ قَدَمٍ	Honey	عَسَلٌ
House	بَيْتٌ	Meat	لَحْمٌ
Milk	حَلِيبٌ	Mosque	مَسْجِدٌ
Motorbike	دَرَّاجَةٌ نَارِيَّةٌ	Notebook	دَفْتَرٌ
Pen	قَلَمٌ	Rice	أُرْزٌ
Shirt	قَمِيصٌ	Table	طَاوِلَةٌ
Tea	شَايٌ	Trouser	سِرْوَالٌ
Train	قِطَارٌ	Water	مَاءٌ

Glossary

Adhān	The call to prayer.
Al-Iqāmah	The call to the establishment of the prayer.
‘Arsh	The Throne of Allāh, it is above the heavens, above all the creation.
‘Awrah	Body parts that must be covered from others.
‘Eid	A day of festival for the Muslims, there are two 'Eids every year, one marking the end of Ramadān and the other in the month of Dhul-Hijjah.
Ākhirah	Hereafter
Āmeen	"O Allāh, answer my supplication."
Āyah (pl: Āyāt)	A verse of the Qur’ān.
Akhlāq	Ettiquetts and manners
Ansār	"Helpers"; the Muslims of Madinah who supported the Muslims who migrated from Makkah.
Bid’ah	A newly invented way in beliefs or actions in the religion which was not done by the Prophet Muhammad ﷺ nor by his Companions.
Deen	The way of life prescribed by Allāh i.e. Islām.
Du’ā	Supplication
Fiqh	The understanding and application of the religion from its sources.

Gheebah	Backbiting
Hadeeth (pl: ahādeeth)	Narration concerning the statements of the Prophet Muhammad ﷺ, his actions, approvals and his attributes.
Halāl	Permitted under the religion.
Harām	Prohibited under the religion.
Imām	The one who leads the prayer.
Jahannam	Hell-Fire
Janazah	Funeral
Jannah	Paradise
Jinn	A creation of Allāh created from smokeless fire.
Jumu'ah	Friday
Khutbah	Sermon
Kufr	Disbelief
Kitaab (pl: Kutub)	Book
Malak (pl: Malā'ikah)	Angel, a creation of Allāh created from light.
Masjid (pl. Masājid)	Mosque
Mu'adhin	The one who calls to prayer.
Muhaajiroon	The Companions who migrated from Makkah to Madinah.

Muslim	A follower of the religion of Islām.
Nabee (pl: Anbiyaa)	Prophet, a man who received revelation from Allāh and ordered to convey it to the people.
Qiblah	The direction the Muslim face during prayer (i.e. towards the K'abah).
Rak'ah	A full unit of prayer containing one Rukoo' and two Sujood.
Rasool	Messenger
Sadaqah	Charity
Sahaabi (pl: Sahaabah)	Companion, a person who met the Prophet Muhammad ﷺ, believing in him and died upon Islām.
Salāh	Prayer
Shaykh	Scholar
Shaytān	Satan
Shirk	Associating partners with Allāh.
Siraat	The Bridge over the Hell-Fire.
Sūrah	A chapter of the Qur'ān.
Takbeer	To say Allāhu Akbar.
Taqwa	Obedience to Allāh, hoping for His mercy upon light from Him and leaving acts of disobedience, out of fear of Him, upon light from Him.
Tashahhud	The portion of the prayer when one sits on the ground facing the Qiblah, glorifying Allāh, and sends peace and prayers upon the Prophet and the righteous people. And says Shahadah.

Tasleem	To say Salām to end and exit the prayer.
Tawheed	Belief that Allāh is the only Lord and the One who deserves to be worshipped alone, who possesses the most beautiful Names and perfect Attributes.
Tayammum	Ablution in the absence of water, performed by wiping clean dust over the hands (to the wrists) and face.
Wudhu	Ablution (ritual washing) that is performed before the prayer and certain other acts of worship.
ﷺ	(Sal Allāhu ‘alaihi wa sallam) May Allāh make good mention of His Prophet in the highest company and grant him safety.
عليه السلام	(‘Alaihis-Salām) Peace be upon him. (Should be said after the name of a Prophet)